NEW TIMES AND OLD ENEMIES

TITLES OF RELATED INTEREST

Resistance through rituals
edited by *Stuart Hall and Tony Jefferson*

Working class culture
edited by *John Clarke et al.*

Back to the future
Philip Cooke

Maps of meaning
Peter Jackson

NEW TIMES
AND
OLD ENEMIES

Essays on cultural studies and America

JOHN CLARKE

Open University

HarperCollins*Academic*

An imprint of HarperCollins*Publishers*

Published by
HarperCollins*Academic*
77-85 Fulham Palace Road
Hammersmith
London W6 8JB
UK

First published in 1991

British Library Cataloguing in Publication Data

Clarke, John
New times and old enemies: Essays on cultural
studies and America.
I. Title
306.0973

ISBN 0–04–445474–0
ISBN 0–04–445473–2 pbk

Library of Congress Cataloging in Publication Data

Applied for

Typeset in 10 on 12 point Sabon
and printed in Great Britain by
Billing and Sons Ltd, London and Worcester

Contents

To Phyl and Frank Clarke
for their encouragement of my wanderings in
new times and new places

Preface

The origins of this book are twofold: first, five months spent in North America during a sabbatical from the Open University in 1986 and, second, my experiences reaching back to my arrival as a postgraduate student in the world of 'cultural studies' in 1972. The sabbatical gave me the opportunity to reflect on long-standing interests in a new cultural, intellectual and political setting. This combination accounts for the peculiarities of the book: it is not a book about 'America', providing a detailed account of its distinctive social structure, culture and politics – my own knowledge is far too slender to provide the basis for such an analysis, nor does it attempt a systematic account of cultural studies as a field, since it is focused on a selection of issues which have particular salience for me.

I suppose it might best be described as an academic travel book, exploring personal preoccupations in new settings. One reviewer suggested that it was an unusually long version of 'What I did on my holidays'. It is, though I have resisted the temptation to use that title. I carried with me a set of interests in cultural studies, and found them revived in trying to make sense of another culture. The result is my attempt to work through some of the central issues of cultural studies using the USA as the source of both new materials and new arguments. Consequently, the book is highly selective in the topics discussed, and has a distinct bias towards coming to grips with contemporary theoretical arguments in cultural analysis. In that sense, it is a highly personal book, reflecting both the aspects of American life that engaged my attention, and the theoretical means at my disposal for making sense of them. Although it is personal, I don't think it is wantonly idiosyncratic, at least to the extent that the issues and arguments with which it is concerned seem to have a wide-ranging and transatlantic currency.

John Clarke

Acknowledgements

The creation of this book has involved me in the accumulation of an enormous number of debts of personal gratitude and a few institutional ones. It would not have been possible without the generosity of the Open University's study-leave arrangements, nor travel grants from the University Travel Committee and the Faculty of Social Sciences' Research Committee. It was also aided by institutional attachments to the Faculty of Human Sciences at the University of Victoria, British Columbia; and the Faculty of Education at the University of Madison-Wisconsin. My exposure to North America was deepened by the variety of invitations to give talks and seminars and by the many people who took the time and trouble to explain their 'America' to me. In particular, I am grateful to those whose hospitality kept me off the 'mean streets' (and out of Holiday Inns): Tony Platt, Suzanne Jonas, Mike Apple, Leslie Roman, John Cossom, Larry Grossberg, Dennis Dworkin, Ian Taylor, Ruth Jamieson, Dick Butsch, Ava Baron, Roy Rosenzweig, Deborah Kaplan, Gord and Cheryl West, Janet Woollacott and Tim Whalley.

The development of the book would not have been possible without people working to keep connections open and correcting the errors of my ways through lengthy correspondence, in particular, Larry Grossberg, Leslie Roman and Allen Hunter. It probably wouldn't have emerged at all without the very patient efforts of two editors at Unwin Hyman: Claire L'Enfant and Sarah Dann.

Finally, I doubt whether I would have survived the experience without the support and care of Les Meyer and Janet Newman, whose friendship makes the Atlantic seem very small indeed. Thanks are not enough.

Acknowledgement is due to the copyright holders for their kind permission to reprint material from the following works:

extracts for *Losing Ground: American Social Policy 1950–1980* by Charles Murray, (1984), are reproduced by permission of Basic Books, Inc., New York; the article appearing in a revised form in this volume as chapter 2 was originally published in the journal *Communication*, and is used by permission of Gordon and Breach Science Publishers S.A., New York.

Introduction

The book is made up of six chapters which originally emerged as essays on particular subjects: class and culture, consumption and the New Right. They are connected in the general sense of being organized around recurrent themes within cultural studies, and more specifically, by being placed in a sequence which seems to have a logic. The book begins with a personal reflection on cultural studies, establishing the core elements of the very British inheritance that I have carried with me on my travels. Chapter 2 records an encounter with theorists of the postmodern condition (the most extreme, or hyper-developed, working out of some of the tendencies in contemporary cultural analysis), whose terminology threatens to become a pervasive influence on cultural analysis. This chapter, described by someone who attended the seminar on which it is based as 'theorised bile', aims to establish the basis for refusing the excesses of postmodernism.

This encounter leads to its mirror opposite: the relationship between Marxist political economy and its analysis of class formation and the domain of culture. Cultural studies has been formed in precisely this tension between the reductionist pressures of orthodox Marxism and the idealist tendency to separate culture from social relations. Chapter 4 pursues this tension into the most visible form of contemporary popular culture – the culture of consumption. The rise of consumer culture upsets many of the theoretical and political orientations based on models of popular culture which have assumed expressive relationships between social groups and their lived cultural practices. In the 1980s, consumption dominated the imagery of popular culture both in the USA and Britain and has become a focal point for cultural analysis.

The rise of consumption has been paralleled by the dominance of the New Right, both in Britain and the USA. Chapter 5 examines some of the ideological and cultural dimensions of the American New Right, particularly its relationship to state welfare. It is directed towards exploring the strengths and limitations of the Gramscian model of hegemony that has played a major role in critical studies of the New Right in Britain. The final chapter offers a conclusion but also reflects the experience of 'bringing it all back home'. My return from a self-confident imperial centre to a society obsessed by the crabby assertion of imperial nostalgia, mining veins of virulent nationalism, nevertheless revealed strong continuities in the central issues of cultural analysis. These were most sharply established in the debate about 'New Times' in the journal *Marxism Today*, which has identified postmodernism, consumer culture, and the rise of the New Right as central constituents of the 'new'. The final chapter also draws together the threads of argument from the earlier chapters through a discussion of the cultural analysis of 'New Times'.

The overall orientation of this book might be summarized in two epigrams. One is from a long-ago student on a course which I was co-tutoring who, after five days of exposure to our variety of cultural analysis, observed: 'Life's just full of contradictions, isn't it?' I have found the comment an indispensable starting point whenever I am asked about my experience of visiting the USA. The second is an equally ironic comment by the Canadian singer–songwriter Bruce Cockburn on the universal politician's claim that 'We'll all get back to normal, if we put our nation first. The trouble with normal is that it always gets worse.'[1] Both comments evoke a truth for me. I hope this book goes some way to explaining why.

NOTES

1 Bruce Cockburn 'The Trouble with Normal', on the LP of the same title, issued by True North Records, and published by Golden Mountain Music Corporation. The song is also available on the compilation LP *Waiting for a Miracle*, FM Records.

1

Cultural studies:
a British inheritance

The intellectual shape of the area of work known as cultural studies owes much to the institutional base provided by the Centre for Contemporary Cultural Studies (CCCS) founded by Richard Hoggart in 1964 (now the Department of Cultural Studies at the University of Birmingham). Hoggart's concern was to create a research centre that would both draw from and transcend the limitations of literary and sociological approaches to culture and would apply this theoretical and methodological synthesis to the study of popular culture. By the end of the 1980s, cultural studies had long transcended these slender origins, having established itself as a subject within British higher education and having spread internationally, both as a theoretical discourse and as a distinctive means of approaching the study of the peculiarities of national cultures. Its intersection with, and insertion into, other academic traditions in different national contexts is beyond the ambitions of this chapter, but would be a fascinating study in the sociology of knowledge or cultural studies.

There are several accounts of the growth and theoretical structure of the field of cultural studies (for example, Hall 1980, Johnson 1979, and Turner, 1990), and this chapter is not intended as a further elaboration of those issues. Instead, I want to draw out some of the ways in which the social practices of the CCCS have shaped the intellectual project of cultural studies. One motive for this chapter is to establish the legacy of cultural studies for me – and for the remaining chapters of this book. It is, therefore, a personal account as well as an intellectual survey, which draws on my experiences of five years as a postgraduate student at the Centre, and on a variety of lingering contacts thereafter.[1]

The impulse for the creation of the CCCS was the publication of Hoggart's *The Uses of Literacy* in 1958. Its exploration of the impact of social change on the patterns of working-class culture established a field (culture) and an intellectual orientation for the new Centre. At the same time, it provided a new, and hitherto unlikely, focal point for the study of culture in British academia: class. The emergent cultural studies drew on, and was fortified by, processes within the existing academic disciplines – processes of dissent, defection and fragmentation. Raymond Williams' devastating critique of 'tradition' in English Literature, and his efforts to emancipate the concept of culture; E. P. Thompson's recovery of the active cultural processes in the 'making' of the English working class; and the shattering of the (American) functionalist hegemony in sociology by the revival of other sociological traditions concerned with meaning and conflict, all provided resources for those concerned with the enterprise of cultural studies.

What the CCCS inherited was a concept – culture – and a range of possibilities. No established field of study nor any accepted theoretical or methodological paradigms existed. The key to the way forward lay in the status of the concept of culture itself. It belonged to no specific academic discipline, yet allowed intellectual access to many: literary criticism, sociology and anthropology in particular. C. Wright Mills once rejected the term as a 'soggy concept', but it was precisely this sogginess that gave cultural studies its intellectual potency. It provided a distinctive point of leverage on many contemporary social issues which were, in other terms, parcelled out to one or other of the academic provinces. It constituted a point of entry through which questions and approaches conventionally excluded could be brought to bear: for example, it permitted qualitative chal-lenges to the quantitative orthodoxy in sociological studies of the mass media. The possession of such a point of entry was vital to the development of cultural studies, emerging in the midst of a tightly structured world of academic disciplines in which the social was tidily delineated into appropriate components and subcomponents. Culture also provided a means of undoing the fragmentation of the social world which such disciplinary proprietorship had as its effect. In these circumstances, the concept of culture carried a complex politics of the emergent cultural studies – an anti-disciplinary academic politics; a totalizing theoretical politics; and a politics of culture itself that aimed to expose the cultural conflicts of contemporary British society for critical study.

After 20 years of expansion in a variety of forms of inter-disciplinary studies, it is more difficult to grasp the weight of ownership which was invested in the disciplinary organization to which the creation of cultural studies represented a threat.[2] Nonetheless, the founding of the CCCS meant that territorial disputes were inevitable, in particular along the borders with English literature and sociology and its attendant subdisciplines. The existence of a group of academics without a tradition, without a clearly demarcated subject matter and methodology rang disciplinary alarm bells and raised the spectre of academic anarchy.

Cultural studies formed a critical point of intersection with other intellectual developments during the 1970s. The foundation of the Centre coincided with the period of fragmentation and internal dissension within the established disciplines. Richard Hoggart himself, together with Raymond Williams, provided focal points within literary studies for the exploration of culture and society. More dramatically, sociology, though not long established as a formal discipline within British academia (Halsey 1987), erupted into internal controversy as radical and critical sociologies flowered during the 1970s, united in their hostility to uncritical empiricism and the theoretical hegemony of American structural functionalism. Such developments created new intellectual resources on which cultural studies could draw (for example the new sociology of deviance contributed to the CCCS's studies of youth subcultures) and new allies located in the established disciplines. The boundary lines were thus blurred from within and without.

Allied to this process was the increasing availability of European social theory and analysis which contributed to the displacement of British and American traditions as the master paradigms of the established disciplines. There is a temptation to equate this process with the wider availability of Marxism (from the founders through to Althusser), but this underestimates, as well as politically misrecognizes, the range of new material which came to hand. Semiology, structuralist anthropology and phenomenology formed significant parts of the import of new theory from Europe alongside new translations of classical and contemporary Marxism. Perry Anderson (1976) and others have commented on Western Marxism's concern with the superstructures of ideology and the state, but again this assessment of Marxist concerns needs to be supplemented by an understanding of the centrality of questions of meaning for the other newly discovered European varieties of analysis. All of these fed into the Centre's attempt to develop cultural analysis, and the absence of an established disciplinary canon undoubtedly meant that such new developments could be appropriated relatively quickly.

Although operating at a less grand theoretical level, the pleasures which accompanied being outside the established disciplines deserve to be mentioned. Being refugees contributed to a shared identity among postgraduate recruits to the Centre and also meant the absence of an inherited position in an established academic hierarchy. The impact of being liberated from serving one's apprenticeship in an existing field formed part of the collective energy of the Centre (and may have contributed to the setting of somewhat grandiose thesis projects). This sense of liberation certainly helped to create a highly productive orientation towards established fields of knowledge. As outsiders, it was possible to approach them as objects of study (rather than as subjects to be absorbed), to raid them for useful knowledge, to criticize their limitations and to juxtapose them with other fields of knowledge to generate new insights and new directions. Relieved of disciplinary responsibility, the Centre aimed for knowledge without frontiers and pursued it across such boundaries with considerable self-confidence (or arrogance).

I have commented on the value of the concept of culture in providing a means of access to other domains of knowledge, but this is only part of its significance. While it was not owned by any of the existing academic disciplines, it was nevertheless bound up in specific political and cultural connotations – in particular, its representation of aesthetic and artistic practice. One essential component of the development of cultural studies was the struggle to liberate culture from these connotations, to make it available as a concept for the analysis of much wider social practices: popular culture. Popular culture, seen both as mass produced cultural forms (popularly consumed) and as popular cultural practices, came to be the terrain which the CCCS staked out against the competing definitions of culture. Predominant amongst these was the idea of High Culture: the product and property of an educated élite, excluding and exclusive. But also to be confronted were ideas of folk culture, the nostalgic antithesis of High Culture, harkening back to an age when the people entertained themselves. Historically juxtaposed with these were conceptions of mass culture, the cultural corollary of mass society theories in sociology, which identified trends towards a culture framed by the opposite poles of private atomization and the anonymous mass of the public realm. Each, in its own way, precluded the conception of an active contemporary popular culture, and each had to be resisted in order to win the space for cultural studies. It is worth noting that the concepts which were developed for the purposes of cultural analysis – of dominant and subordinate meanings and struggle and resistance – are also the most apposite ones in describing the intellectual politics of the Centre's development.

BASE AND SUPERSTRUCTURE

The Centre provided an institutional basis for the development of cultural studies though of a relatively slender kind. Formally, its academic resources were minimal. At the time of my arrival in 1972, its staff consisted of one and a half members of academic staff (Stuart Hall, acting as director during Hoggart's absence at UNESCO, and Michael Green) and one secretary (Joan Goode).[3] Supplementing these was a small independent library, some offices, several typewriters and a stencil machine, together with a group of full- and part-time postgraduate students. In crudely material terms, this constituted a very tiny base, however, as all non-reductionist Marxists know (or at least knew), it is not the technical means of production which are the determining force, but the social relations of production – and the Centre developed a very distinctive set of social relations of intellectual production.

The most distinctive element was an overarching commitment to collective work. This was a self-conscious rejection of the conventional mode of organizing postgraduate labour, and reflected one effect of wider cultural politics on the development of the Centre. In this instance, the late 1960s' interest in communal and collective forms of self-determination provided a basis for an alternative to the conventionally individualized and hierarchical modes of academic life. The collectivity as a whole was involved in the development of cultural studies, both in the general sense, and, through the structure of subgroups, working on particular fields, such as literature, media, women's studies, subcultures, the state and so on. Each subgroup took responsibility for its own development and direction and for the presentation of regular work in progress reports to the other members of the Centre.[4] At the more general level, the work of the subgroups was supplemented by a general theory seminar and regular visiting speakers. This commitment to collective practice also extended to the organization of the Centre, with general business discussed at a weekly meeting open to all members of the Centre, and specific areas being allocated to a range of administrative subgroups.

This collective pattern of work underpinned the Centre's high level of productivity, although it shared many of the problems characteristic of efforts to build collective organizations. It was possible for too ready an assumption of a unity of interests to be developed leading to a marginalization of competing concerns. The most significant, but not the only, examples of this are the internal politics which surrounded the development of groups working on women and race within the Centre, both of which had to challenge their exclusion from the core of cultural studies in both theoretical and political terms (see CCCS 1978: 7–18; CCCS 1982: 7–8). Equally, the practice of collaborative writing could be highly contested, difficult and long drawn out, while collective projects could displace the individual thesis projects on which people were engaged. In spite of such problems, the commitment to collective work was maintained and, for most people at the Centre, overcame the characteristic postgraduate experiences of isolation and anomie. The existence of collective projects generated a strong sense of common purpose and identity together with an obligation to produce – at least for the regular work in progress reports to the other members of the Centre, and beyond that for the Centre's journal and occasional papers series. Associated with this obligation was a strong emphasis on generating written material. Individuals and groups were encouraged to write down their work in progress from an early stage as a prerequisite of collective discussion and criticism. Here, too, the Centre's practice worked against some of the characteristic postgraduate experiences, where writing is confined to the production of a thesis and is generally produced solely for the eyes of the thesis' supervisor and examiners. For students at the Centre, this may have reduced some of the pressures which are associated with more individualized experiences of writing. Writing was also less highly charged because of the provisional quality. It was always a record of a stage of work in progress rather than a finished product. This sense was captured in the title adopted for the Centre's journal: *Working Papers in Cultural Studies*.[5] Although the journal was subsequently succeeded by a series of books published by Hutchinson (and, following the vagaries of market forces in publishing, taken over by Unwin Hyman, and most recently by Harper Collins) the provisional and exploratory quality has remained a significant feature of the Centre's work. I do not mean that such work is marked by tentativeness or an excess of reticence. On the contrary, much of the writing reflects a high level of confidence both in the critiques of other positions offered and in the alternatives being advanced. Nevertheless, there is a persistent sense of areas of study and theoretical arguments being 'opened up' rather than closed off.

THE PRACTICE OF CRITIQUE

The intellectual project of the CCCS – the development of cultural studies – gave rise to specific modes of intellectual work as well as involving particular types of social relations. At the heart of these lay the practice of critique – the subjection of existing knowledge to critical interrogation to generate new insights. Such a process was essential for the construction of a new field of study whose subject matter existed within the domains of other academic disciplines. Within this critical practice, the Centre adopted a version of what Althusser termed 'symptomatic reading': the analysis of texts for their 'silences' as much as for their statements with a view to revealing their underlying problematics. Such readings involved 'privileging' developing positions within cultural studies as a vantage point from which to examine and assess other positions. I stress developing positions since the practice of critique also fed back into the further elaboration of cultural analysis, rather than being a process of criticism from a pre-given or finished standpoint in cultural theory.

In the study of youth subcultures (Hall and Jefferson, eds, 1976), the development of a cultural analysis of youth began from a critique of existing studies of youth within sociology and psychology. The critique had two main axes: one was to question the assumed primacy of age as a social relation, examining the suppression of class relations in favour of generational ones (and insisting on relational rather than hierarchical conceptions of class). The other was to privilege the sphere of culture, viewed as a domain of active social practice involving the construction of meaning. Thus youth subcultures emerged as objects of study: social 'texts' to be decoded through an analysis of the intersection of class and generational cultural practices. But the means of conducting such cultural analysis were only developed in the process of that critique, rather than providing its starting point. The subcultures group did not possess a pre-given model of class and age relations. The aim of its work was to develop such a model, which required the construction of concepts of class cultural and subcultural practice at the same time as the deconstruction of generationally based theories of youth. In this sense, each of the subgroup fields within the Centre was simultaneously engaged in the construction of new approaches to a specific area of study and to the elaboration of theoretical models which fed back into the wider conception of cultural studies itself.

This linking of particular areas of study to the more general theoretical problems of cultural studies meant that the development of theoretical work at the Centre had a particular character. The working up of theories of culture rarely took place solely at an abstract level, since new theories and concepts were constantly being set against the problems involved in analysing particular cultural fields. The diversity of the subgroup regions, and their relative autonomy, meant that their contributions to the overall development of cultural studies kept open the theoretical dimension of cultural analysis, since different theoretical emphases were developed and brought to bear in each of the subgroups.

This uneven development between the subgroups combined with the absence of an established field of cultural studies to ensure a high level of theoretical openness in the work of the Centre – a readiness to take on new possibilities from a wide range of sources: anthropology; semiotics; critical or radical sociology; the new social history; structuralism; Marxism and feminism. But this willingness to explore new directions was never merely a following of theoretical fashion, nor solely a search for theory for its own sake. The dangers of trendiness and theoreticism, both of which have been criticisms levelled at the Centre, certainly existed, and occasionally threatened to divert the development of cultural studies into an epistemological nirvana, or paralyse the pursuit of substantive analysis through the prospect of infinite regress to still more abstract levels of inquiry. But for the most part, the engagement with theory was selective, searching out those which could contribute to the understanding of cultural forms and cultural practices. More importantly, the taking up of new theoretical directions usually involved a sense of distance: an effort to appropriate good sense without wholesale adoption. Once again, this involved the practice of critique: the interrogation of theories and positions to see what they would reveal, together with an attempt to apply them to substantive areas of analysis and to test them against the problems of cultural studies (see the discussion in Hall 1988).

The effect of attempting to maintain this critical relationship to new theoretical work can be seen in the history of the Centre's work. This is not a history of linear development, punctuated by great leaps forward or, more painfully still, epistemological ruptures, in which each succeeding theoretical innovation displaces its predecessors as the new orthodoxy. Such a view of periodized stages misses crucial aspects of the Centre's work. The practice of theoretical critique within the CCCS resisted the installation of any one theoretical hegemony: appropriations of new theoretical directions were woven alongside (sometimes with the seams still showing), rather than displacing, previous models. So traces of different theoretical approaches can be found held in suspension alongside one another. This is a considerable distance from formalistic models of 'paradigm shifts' or even the view of 'theoretical practice' as schematized by Althusser as the application of Generalities II to Generalities I to produce Science (Generalities III) (Althusser 1970: 89–90). Thus, *Resistance through Rituals* (Hall and Jefferson, eds, 1976) bears the marks of Lévi-Strauss alongside political sociology; 'labelling theory' alongside Althusser; and semiotics alongside Gramsci. Insights won from particular positions remained in place as useful knowledge even while new directions were being explored. There remains no single theory or model of cultural studies which exercises dominance over the field – in more recent times, Derrida, Lacan, Foucault and postmodernism have been the subjects of new critical engagements.

This theoretical untidiness has proved a source of frustration to commentators on, and critics of, the work of the CCCS, since it makes it difficult to identify a 'Birmingham School' with a unified theoretical and methodological approach to cultural studies. Convenient though such designations are in the currency of academic discourse, there is little evidence that the Centre ever aspired to, much less achieved, a unified theoretical position or approved methodology. Certainly, the internal experience of both the unfinished quality of the work and the ferment of mutual criticism and argument was always sharply at odds with external perceptions of a Centre orthodoxy. One of the most visible testaments to the shifting forms of the Centre's work can be found in the changing articulations between class and culture.

THE RISE AND FALL OF CLASS CULTURE

The early development of cultural studies was overshadowed by the 'problem of the working class'. Richard Hoggart's exploration of the impact of mass culture on the traditional practices of working-class life in *The Uses of Literacy* (1958) was only one part of a much wider concern with the fate of the British working class in the 1950s and 60s. Both in the social sciences and in fictional representations, the future of the class in the face of affluence, the restructuring of British capitalism and the impact of a collectivist welfare state seemed to hold the key to understanding the dynamics of social change in postwar Britain (Critcher 1979; Laing 1985). Given the Hoggartian inheritance and the wider cultural conditions, it is no surprise that cultural studies first took shape around the problems of the relationship between class and culture.

This starting point established two of the characteristic tensions that became embedded in the development of cultural studies. The first was the struggle to establish the right to speak of class in relation to culture at all. Culture had to be liberated as a concept from the ties which bound it to forms of analysis which refused the idea of class: the conceptions of culture dominant in literature, anthropology and sociology. In the last of these, the struggle was a double one. On the one hand, class had to be asserted against the homogenizing perspectives of mass society and mass culture. On the other hand, a more active sense of class as a social force had to be developed against the British tradition of treating class as a social classification: the hierarchy of lower, middle and upper, with all their infinite gradations. The search for this dynamic linkage of class and culture led inexorably to the second characteristic tension of cultural studies – the relationship with Marxism. Marxism offered a tradition of thought which had the connection between class and the twin concepts of ideology and consciousness at its centre. The Centre's encounter with Marxism was to run the full gamut of Marxist conceptualizations of the relationship between being and consciousness: from *The German Ideology*'s 'the ruling ideas of the age are the ideas of the ruling class', through *Capital*'s suggestions of the connection between 'real relations and phenomenal forms' and Althusser's 'ideology as an imaginary relation', to Gramsci's cryptic commentaries on hegemony and common sense (CCCS 1977).

This relationship was never an easy one. Marxism offered the promise of linking class and culture. At the same time, it presented the threat of submerging the specificity of the cultural in the tendency to reductionism: the view that consciousness, ideology or culture is an inscribed characteristic of class position.

The Centre's work involved a constant effort to keep open and think through the domain of the cultural: to explore what Althusser termed its 'relative autonomy'. In the process, this necessitated uneasy and critical relationships with almost every formulation of ideology, culture and consciousness. Some of these took place around what might be termed the axis of materialism and idealism: how to insist on the specificity of symbolic orders while maintaining their determinate connection to the social relations of class. Others took place around the axis of culturalism and structuralism: how to insist that culture was the product of social practice by social actors without falling from the tightrope between the humanism of knowing subjects and the functionalism of self-reproducing structures (Johnson 1979).

The difficulties of this relationship explain why cultural studies never completely closed around Marxism, in spite of Marxism's dominant position as a theoretical resource. Spaces were always held open for non-Marxist approaches which were focused on the symbolic order thereby providing a counterweight to the reductionist dangers of Marxism. This tension explains the apparent survivals of the Centre's pre-Marxist history (semiotics, anthropology) as well as the more recent excursions into the Foucauldian realm of discourse and the domain of subjectivity. I do not mean to underestimate the other theoretical and political forces which contributed to the development of such concepts as alternatives to Marxist analysis: feminism, in particular has inspired a long and varied struggle to displace the presumptions of a Marxist hegemony within cultural studies (CCCS 1978; Roman *et al.* eds, 1988; and Stacey *et al.*, eds, forthcoming), but I also think it is important not to over-read the density of the relationship between cultural studies and Marxism as if Marxism were the only, rather than the dominant intellectual force in cultural studies.

Nevertheless, this protracted engagement with Marxism led to the development of a cultural studies at whose centre stood the issues of class struggle, domination, subordination and resistance conducted through cultural practice. These concerns, although worked through in different ways, form a coherent strand linking such substantive areas as youth subcultures, the transition from school to work, the mass media, the education system, crime and the justice system and the development of the British state. The theoretical problem embedded in each of the substantive areas was that of how to construct a non-reductionist analysis of class and culture, that would transcend the conception of a class culture that directly expressed the interests, or world view, of its originating class position. It was this impetus towards a view of culture as a site of struggle for domination (rather than the conflict of different cultural essences) that helped to revive the discarded notion of popular culture.

At an earlier phase of the development of cultural studies, popular culture had proved a relatively unsatisfactory concept. It was imprecise: at one and the same time evoking echoes of folk culture, ideas of the people and their self-made amusements and the rapid growth of the popularly consumed pleasures of the mass media. Its imprecision seemed to render it inadequate as a concept around which to organize the field of cultural studies, and at the same time, seemed to mask the very class relations and practices which cultural studies was working to reveal. As a concept, then, it appeared mystificatory rather than relevatory. The loosening of the direct linkage of class and culture come through Marxist analyses of the realm of ideology which highlighted the non-class specific forms of representation. This had its foundations in Althusser's exploration of ideology with its emphasis on the interpellation of subjects as individuals, and was enhanced by Poulantzas' consideration of the terrain of the 'national-popular' as the ideological realm involved in the formation of non-class social identities (Althusser 1971; Poulantzas 1979). In cultural studies, these attacks on 'expressive' conceptions of class consciousness coincided with the growing interest in Gramsci's concepts of hegemony and common sense, which also directed attention to the cultural struggles of domination and subordination in the formation of national-popular cultures (although with a more concrete and historically specific focus than Althusser or Poulantzas).[6]

Overlaying these developments was the growing social, political and academic salience of non-class forms of social divisions: in particular, those of race and gender. Both led to profound critiques of the existing social and intellectual practices of cultural studies from within and outside of CCCS. At issue was the theoretical hegemony of class as the dominant relation to be analysed in cultural studies (for example, CCCS 1978 and CCCS 1982). Both these critiques generated new theoretical arguments about the formation of culture and new substantive analyses of the formation of British culture. In doing so, they opened up new domains of cultural formations and practice for analysis. They decentred class as the focal problematic of cultural studies, and established continuing arguments about the articulation of class, gender and race and about the politics of difference in the processes of cultural formation. One effect of these initiatives was the enrichment of the concept of popular culture as well as an insistence on the complexity of relations of dominance and subordination to be discerned within it. (See, for example, Roman *et al.*, eds, 1988; Gilroy 1987; and Stacey *et al.*, eds, forthcoming.)

Complexly interwoven with these developments was the explosion of post-Althusserian theorizing about ideology and culture. The Althusserian moment, for all its problems, liberated the concept of ideology from its essentialist and reductionist connotations and established the conditions for a number of new directions. So, the connection between ideology, interpellation and subjectivity which Althusser exposed created the space for the development of analyses of language and subjectivity and revived connections between cultural analysis and psychoanalysis through the linking figure of Lacan (many of the essays in Parts 3 and 4 of CCCS 1980 explore these issues). This terrain proved to be a fertile ground for the creation of links between cultural studies and some varieties of feminist analysis, particularly around the concern with contradictory subjectivity as a nexus for linking the ideological production of subjects and the domain of the personal. In other directions, these post-Althusserian concerns also opened up new points of contact with forms of textual analysis of popular cultural forms in film and television (for example, in the journal *Screen*), which explored the processes of subject positioning and production. Perhaps the most potent occupier of these post-Althusserian spaces has been the Foucauldian concept of 'discourse' which simultaneously attacked the reductionist tendencies of Marxism and offered an approach which linked the production of knowledge, subjectivities and power. Foucault's challenge to Marxism's privileging of class (and the mode of production) and its monistic and over-centralized concept of power, combined with his focus on the production of subjects, underpins the pertinence of the knowledge–power nexus as an alternative to a Marxist cultural analysis, particularly for those concerned with gender and sexuality. (Beechey and Donald eds, 1985, offer an overview of many of these post-Althusserian developments.)

This proliferation of discourses about culture, ideology and knowledge has opened up cultural studies both theoretically and in the range of substantive areas of analysis. In the process, the earlier concern with class cultures has been decentred, both from within Marxism and from without. In its place are more differentiated and contradictory conceptions of cultural politics. It is in this context that the idea of popular culture has returned to a more central role in cultural studies. Minimally, popular culture has emerged as a term describing the field within which competing perspectives can locate their objects of study and which carries no specific weighting to any one set of social relations, although still leaving open considerable ground for dispute about the articulation (or non-articulation) of those different relations. It embraces a more differentiated understanding of the people and their constitution through a politics of difference than an approach which sought merely to demystify the concealment of class relations in popular forms. Popular culture (or more precisely the national-popular culture) has also been taken up as the focus for Gramscian-influenced analyses of ideology and common sense: the terrain on which the struggle for hegemony is conducted (Hall 1981, Laclau 1977, Bennett 1986 a and b).

CULTURAL STUDIES: THE LEGACY

In the 1980s cultural studies became a firmly established part of the academic scene both in Britain and elsewhere. It has now grown and diversified – both in its range of subject matter and in the variety of theoretical perspectives which are deployed within it. The Centre, too, has survived a difficult period to arrive at a more secure footing as the Department of Cultural Studies at the University of Birmingham. After 25 years it exercises a less dominant role over the field than in its early years, but its legacy for the theory and practice of cultural studies is a substantial one. In this final section, I want to lay claim to my share of that inheritance.

The Centre's commitment to collective work continues to act as an example of how to resist the individualized and privatized practices which still dominate the mode of academic production. Painful and troublesome as it often could be, the attempt to build cooperative modes of working was both productive and enriching in its own right and also highlighted the limitations of conventional academic work, especially in postgraduate study which remains locked in the habits of extremely unsplendid isolation. I have been fortunate to work in one of the places where forms of collaborative work have been developed: the Open University, whose course teams, rather than individual lecturers, form the unit of academic production. Indeed, until now, my own writing has tended to be of a collaborative nature, and has been both more productive and more enjoyable for being so.[7]

Of equal significance is the complexity which lay at the heart of cultural studies from its very origins: the profound, if profoundly ambiguous, interleaving of attention to culture as lived experience and as texts. This tension, emerging from the attempt to synthesize the literary and anthropological senses of culture, has been a formative and highly productive one for the field. There has been a constant temptation to fragment the problem of culture, separating the study of discourses or texts from the practices of cultural subjects, precisely because the task of holding onto both elements is so difficult. On the textual wing, there has been a tendency to dissolve the tension by dealing with subject positions rather than subjects. This leaves to one side the difficult question of the actual efficacy or productivity of the text–discourse and reads only the intended effect on the ideal subject projected within the text–discourse. In some instances, this has involved an elision between the subject position and the subject, as if texts do produce their subjects in a vacuum, separated from either other texts or other social relations. On the other wing, that of lived experience, there is a temptation to homogenize the situated culture of subjects and treat texts–discourses as the external impositions of an alien culture such that the situated culture provides the raw materials of resistance. This reconstructs the separation of dominant and subordinate cultures and the danger of essentialist or expressive views of culture.[8]

For me, this tendency towards separation is why the Gramscian-derived framework of hegemony–ideology–common sense remains the most productive approach to be constructed within cultural studies. It sustains the early cultural studies concern with culture as the site of struggles for domination and subordination while offering a means of preventing the slide into essentialism and reductionism. But it also situates particular areas of substantive analysis within a more totalizing structure of political issues and resists the tendency to fragment cultural studies into different – and separate – domains. Nevertheless, the totality which it presents is one of a unity-in-difference rather than an expressive totality – no single organizing social or economic principle governs it. It emphasizes the salience of cultural practice through its non-functionalist view of domination and resistance. Hegemony has to be worked for, being neither a pre-given property of economic, social or political power nor a stable condition which, once achieved, is unchangeable (Hall 1988 and 1989).[9] In these ways, the Gramscian approach to hegemony seems to me to sustain the strengths of cultural studies and minimize some of the weaknesses.

Finally, I want to stress the importance of the experience of being shaped by a field of study which was never finished – where the dominant sense was of work always being in progress. As I've suggested earlier, this open-ended quality has its roots in the tensions which were part of the constitution of cultural studies as an academic area: its non-disciplinary character, its boundary disputes with other disciplines and its constant opening of new possibilities. This character also finds echoes in Gramsci's work, both in the provisional quality of his analysis and in his insistence that conjunctures – historical moments – need to be investigated rather than have their shape deduced from abstract theoretical principles.

For me, these elements – the attempts to develop collective practice, to live productively with analytical tensions rather than magically resolving them, and to sustain open-endedness in the face of temptations to solidify theoretical positions – form the good sense of cultural studies. They have had a profound influence on me and I hope that their traces can be found in the rest of this book.

NOTES

This chapter is based on a seminar given at Carleton University, Ottawa, in April 1986 in which I was invited to provide a 'personal retrospective' on the Centre for Contemporary Cultural Studies. I am grateful to Ian Taylor and Peter Bruck for the invitation, and to all those who took part for helping me to think about my inheritance. Its development has also been aided by comments from Larry Grossberg and Janet Newman.

1   I was a student at the CCCS between 1972 and 1977. Subsequently, I completed co-editing *Working Class Culture* with Chas Critcher and Richard Johnson; contributed to a book of essays on the British State between 1880 and 1930 (Langan and Schwarz eds, 1987); and co-authored a book on leisure with another ex-CCCS member, Chas Critcher (Clarke and Critcher 1985).

2   I have never been able to decide whether cultural studies is best described as inter-, multi- or cross-disciplinary. I suspect that the most appropriate term is undisciplined, in the positive sense that the work is not confined by established disciplinary practices and conventions. I suspect that many of its critics would accept the term for its more pejorative connotations.

3   The academic staffing of the Centre was subsequently expanded, peaking at three members of staff: Stuart Hall, Michael Green and Richard Johnson. Maureen McNeil joined the Centre on Stuart Hall's departure to the Open University. They were intermittently supplemented by externally funded Research Fellows: Paul Willis and Chris Griffin.

4   This is, of course, different from the place of postgraduates in the research team model practised in some areas of science and technology, where the student is a junior member, researching a specified part of the senior academic's field of work.

5   The journal involved a typical Centre pattern of craft production, being produced in house by a combination of editorial and production groups with only printing being under taken externally. The production of pamphlets and occasional papers followed a similar pattern, but without outside printing.

6   The productive combination of these Althusserian and Gramscian concerns underpinned the explorations of Englishness and the British state in *Policing the Crisis* (Hall *et al.* 1979), and prefigured much subsequent analysis of Thatcherism (for example, Hall 1989).

7 Indeed, the main difficulty of producing this book has been to find a way of substituting for the presence of co-authors who will take apart my carefully honed sentences to create sense, as well as to provide the obligation and discipline to keep working. It will be clear that I haven't yet found a satisfactory alternative.

8 I realize these comments are somewhat overdrawn, but think that they do identify two contrasting means of resolving the tension in cultural studies. Roman *et al.* eds, 1988, present both a vigorous critique of this tendency to separation, and an attempt to re-synthesize the two elements. Clarke 1990 examines some of the political implications of this tension.

9 I have often thought that the Gramscian contribution to cultural studies could be summarized in the injunction to use the verb 'to attempt' in every key sentence as an index of cultural struggle and the non-functional quality of hegemony. For example, 'Thatcherism *attempted to* form a new ideological hegemony by its selective addressing of common-sense...'.

2

Enter the Cybernauts: problems in postmodernism

The arrival of theories of postmodernism threatens to unleash yet another spiral of argument, theoretical debate and analysis within that loosely bounded field known as critical theory. It raises new theoretical and epistemological issues to be wrangled over, offers new standpoints for engaging in the analysis of texts, apparatuses of communication, and the 'constitution of subjectivities'. In what follows I will argue that to pursue this further twist in the spiral is an intellectually and politically erroneous path, no matter how exhilarating the attractions of sliding around on such a new theoretical surface may feel. The first problem for any such argument is how to accomplish a simplified definition of what postmodernism is: a problem exacerbated both by the variety of designations of postmodernism, and the way in which the postmodernists themselves present their project in a postmodernist manner: elusive – allusive, full of slides, slippages, and disjunctures.

While accepting that postmodernism is often located by reference to certain aesthetic practices in for example, literature, television, or architecture, I think there are two broader fields to which it lays claim in trying to demonstrate the existence of a postmodern condition. These are the interconnected fields of contemporary culture (or, more analytically, contemporary signifying practice) and contemporary subjectivity. In terms of contemporary signifying practice, the postmodern condition is identified as one in which knowledge and meaning have been fragmented and dislocated. It is a condition in which scratch music, jump cut editing, non-narrative and non-realist forms of representation are characteristic. It is a condition of the juxtaposition of arbitrary signs, and of the effects of irony, pastiche, recycling and reiteration. To put it a little more concretely, it is a condition of being condemned to watch endless re-runs of *Miami Vice* without being able to tell the difference between one episode and another. For me, the possibility of a postmodern condition was summed up by two experiences: first, watching television when the President of the USA's announcement that 'surgical strikes' on Libya had been carried out was followed by an advertisement for incontinence underwear; and secondly, reading Jean-François Lyotard's *The Postmodern Condition* (1984) in a BurgerKing restaurant.

But postmodernism is also an analysis of the condition of contemporary subjectivity, a condition which mirrors that of signifying practice. We (the postmodern subjects) are cut adrift from the master-narratives of history which previously functioned to locate subjects and to give meaning. Instead, we are now subjects created by fragments of knowledge and meaning: bewildered, bemused, betrayed or schizophrenic, lost in the fragments or simply plugged into the terminal. Most importantly, we are not only all these things and more, we are also loving it: awash in what Baudrillard has called the 'ecstasy of communication'. This point references the third theme in postmodernism: the apparatus which articulates the new practices of signification with the new condition of fragmented subjectivity. The technological transformations of the means of communication, with their enhanced powers of speed, penetration and dominance have structurally reordered (or disordered) the world, collapsing time and space into an instantaneous succession of communicative instants. Arthur Kroker offers this description of how modernist assumptions have been inverted in the new epoch

TV is, in a very literal sense, the real world, not of modern but of post modern culture, society and economy – of society driven by the spirit of *technicisme* triumphant and of real popular culture driven onwards by the ecstasy and decay of the obscene spectacle – and that everything which escapes the real world of TV, everything which is not videated by its identity principle, everything which is not processed through TV as the technical apparatus of relational power *par excellence* is peripheral to the main tendencies of the contemporary century. (1985: 38.)

Baudrillard (1983) expresses the same approach more simply, if more enigmatically, in the proposition that 'reality flickers'. Postmodernism is complex because contained within it are presciptions for an aesthetic, signifying practice, a description of contemporary culture and a theorization of the conditions of contemporary culture. In what follows, I shall be taking issue with the last of these elements because I believe that we have arrived at 'the end of History' (the postmodern condition) via a particular theoretical route rather than through a real historical journey. To put this another way, postmodernism can appear as the (il)logical next step in contemporary critical theorizing, because it rests on certain theoretical preconditions which are already well established. In the world of post-everything-theorizing (post-Marxist, post-structuralist and post-feminist), postmodernism lays claim to an array of epistemological and theoretical assumptions which we now hold to be self-evident truths – and takes them to excess. Postmodernism, then, appears uncomfortably familiar because of its ability to recycle concepts and propositions already in play. Consequently, it is securely placed within the inflationary spiral of contemporary critical theorizing, although, to borrow ironically from another discourse, 'stagflation' might be a more accurate designation of this condition.

Because of this interconnection, I want to proceed by considering a number of themes and concepts established in critical theorizing and examine the postmodernist appropriation of them. In doing so, I shall be posing what might be termed vulgar materialist objections to them, in order to consider the potential basis for a properly materialist alternative for analysing the complex world of contemporary capitalism. I think that this procedure is worth undertaking to clarify some of the central glissades – those slippages of theoretical legerdemain – performed before our very eyes by these theoretical wizards (and the occasional witch).[1]

CAN YOU EAT A MENU?
OR, WHAT IS A COMMODITY?

I choose to begin with the problem of the commodity for two reasons. First, it is where Baudrillard, in his book *For a critique of the political economy of the sign* (1981), began his epic journey to the terminal. And second, back in pre-history, it was Marx's starting point for unravelling the mysteries of the capitalist mode of production. The conjuncture of these two points of departure is not accidental.

For Baudrillard, his reanalysis of the commodity allowed two epochal conclusions to be drawn. The first was that the commodity is a Sign: it signifies. The commodity form is ideological both in the sense which Marx recognized, the form of exchange value (the fetishism of the commodity), and in a sense which Marx failed to grasp, its particular objective form: its use value. Baudrillard argues that Marx missed the ideological character of use value, leaving it to refer to a non-ideological realm of 'needs' which were accounted for either by a trans-historical speculative anthropology (human nature) or, what is worse, a historical–cultural relativism. To use either of these referents to account for the consumption of commodities is, for Baudrillard, to enter the realm of ideology, according to the following (much abbreviated) argument. There are no subjects (in the post-Althusserian theoretical world) who are not the product of a signifying practice (substitute 'ideologically interpellated' or 'discursively constituted' at will) and therefore there are no needs which are not discursively constituted. Commodities are signs which signify the needs which they are intended to fulfil, therefore use value is already pre-given, inscribed in the signifying practice of the commodity itself. Consequently the commodity satisfies the need which it has created. Consumption, then, is the consummation of the subject's insertion into ideology.

I shall return to the subject of subjects in a moment, but first I want to note a couple of points about the commodity. The commodity does signify, but it does not only signify. It is also an object requiring a labour of consumption with particular material effects. If we take the most vulgar case, I am uncertain how Baudrillard subsists if he is unable to distinguish food objects (which may also signify) from signs (which may represent food objects). Unless there is a new neurological relation which permits direct food intake from BurgerKing ads, I want to insist that there is a material difference between the menu and the objects which it represents.

I wish to pursue the relationship between the commodity and use value a little further, because once one leaves a very high level of theoretical abstraction, there is a discovery to be made. This is that commodities seem to be imperfectly articulated with needs. Commodities and their consumption do not exist in the sort of direct relationship suggested by Baudrillard's argument: on the contrary, many commodities fail to realize their exchange value (that is, they are not sold). Capitalism remains a system which is characterized by crises of over production: there are, to borrow from the language of information technology, still a few bugs in the system. There are two conditions which need to be taken into account in understanding this imperfect articulation of production and consumption. On the one hand, the consuming subject is not solely constituted by the signifying practices of consumption, but also by other ideologies and by being embedded in sets of social relationships which may generate a more complex array of needs than can be contained within the array of signs available in the market-place. On the other hand, consumption, although it is often difficult to discern in postmodern theorizing, still includes an economic relation. The price has to be paid to enter the palace of consumption. Minimally, needs are articulated to commodities through money, and the wage (or its substitutes) remains a matter of social conflict (indexed by the recent attempts by American capital to persuade its workers to 'give back' part of their wage packets).

This is not to suggest that there exists a perfectly worked out theory of needs that could be substituted for the abolition of use value and the materiality of the commodity in postmodern theorizing. But nor do I accept that, because a difficult problem exists, the solution is to write it out by reference to its discursive constitution. There is one further slide in the commodity-which-signifies discussion which is worth drawing attention to. Having started from the object (the commodity), and identified it as an object which signifies, Baudrillard's analysis thereafter proceeds as if it is only a sign. The object itself disappears from view – is de-materialized – leaving only its sign for analysts to wrangle over. This abolition of the object in Baudrillard is only a special case of a much more general practice in recent critical theory, which might be termed the paradox of the materialization of the sign and the de-materialization of everything else.[2] This more general case is at the core of issues about ideology, discourse and the subject.

LOOK, NO HANDS:
OR, BACK TO THE SUBJECT

Implicit in the attack on use value and the material character of the commodity is the wider process of the 'abolition of the subject' in critical theorizing (in the empiricist sense of the 'knowing' subject or the metaphysical sense of the 'subject of history'). I have no great interest in reiterating 15 years of the decentring and deconstruction of the subject in critical theory, so suffice it to say that, in the post-Althusserian world, such a subject is unimaginable except as an ideological effect, in that the effect of ideology is to interpellate individuals as if they were unitary knowing subjects. In (theoretical) reality, however, the subject is effectively a contradictory subject, constituted out of the cross-cutting interpellations of a plurality of ideologies – discourses (producing legal subjects, political subjects, gendered subjects, and so on).

In what follows, I do not mean to seem uncharitable about certain important theoretical arguments, particularly the insistence by Althusser and through semiology that signs and ideologies are materialized, through social practices, in gestures, sounds, writing, images, and so forth. These seem to me to be necessary correctives to idealist views of ideology as ideas. However, something peculiar has happened thereafter. Having established the material quality of ideology, everything else we had hitherto thought of as material has disappeared. There is nothing outside of ideology (or discourse). Where Althusser was concerned with ideology as the imaginary relation of subjects to the real relations of their existence, the connective quality of this view of ideology has been dissolved because it lays claim to an outside, a real, an extra-discursive for which there exists no epistemological warrant without lapsing back into the bad old ways of empiricism or metaphysics.[3] The same disconnection has been conducted on the sign in semiological analysis. Where it used to contain a relation between the signifier (the representation) and the signified (the referent), anti-empiricism has taken the formal arbitrariness of the connection between the signifier and signified and replaced it with the abolition of the signified (there can be no real objects out there, because there is no out there for real objects to be). Thereafter, meaning came to depend upon the place of the signifier in a chain of signifiers (meaning through difference), and postmodernism has proclaimed the final step: the disruption of the chain, the collapse of difference and the emergence of indifference.

In Lyotard (1984), we find this slippage or elision of other material conditions being conducted in relation to his preferred version of postmodernism – the centrality of linguistic relations and their articulation with the fragmentation of knowledge and meaning. Early in *The Postmodern Condition*, he introduces the concept of 'language games' as a social relation:

> It should now be clear from which perspective I chose lan-guage games as my general methodological approach. I am not claiming that the entirety of social relations is of this nature – that will remain an open question. But there is no need to resort to some fiction of social origins to establish that language games are the minimum relation required for society to exist. (1984: 15.)

Passing over whether language games are the minimum neces-sary for society to exist, let us pursue Lyotard's handling of this 'open question' as to whether language exhausts the entirety of social relations. Some 25 pages later in the text, we come to the following sentence: 'The social bond *is* linguistic, but is not woven with a single thread.' (1984: 40; emphasis added), and the open question has conveniently disappeared. Worse follows when Lyotard comes to discuss the role of 'force' in the social relation: 'Whenever efficiency (that is, obtaining the desired effect) is derived from a "Say or do this, or you'll never speak again", then we are in the realm of terror, and the social bond is destroyed.' (1984: 46.) I can think of few more striking indicators of the political and intellectual impoverishment of a view of society that can only recognize the discursive. If the worst terror we can envisage is the threat not to be allowed to speak, we are appallingly ignorant of terror in its elaborate contemporary forms. It may be the intellectual's conception of terror (what else do we do but speak?), but its projection onto the rest of the world would be calamitous – if the rest of the world took it seriously.

Still, let me try to suggest some vulgar objections which might, however tenuously, provide some theoretical underpinning for the moral outrage which such a parlous conception of terror creates in me. I think that expressed in postmodernism is a peculiar inversion of one of the central metaphors of early industrial capitalism. Where capitalists wanted workers for their hands (and, indeed, referred to them as such), and thought of their heads as redundant, postmodernists want us for our heads, and think of the body as redundant:

> This is the time of miniaturization, telecommand and the microprocession of time, bodies, pleasures . . . What remains are only concentrated effects, miniaturized and immediately available. This change for human scale to a system of nuclear matrices is visible everywhere: this body, our body, often appears simply superfluous, basically useless in its extension, in the mutliplicity and complexity of its organs, its tissues and its functions, since today everything is concentrated in the brain and in genetic codes which alone sum up the operational definition of being. (Baudrillard, 1983: 129.)

The body, however continues to be a source of troubling thoughts to me, it remains stubbornly (and grossly) material. It also constitutes a form of bounding to the variety of subjectivities which present themselves to me: some of them simply cannot be materialized. Equally, the body persists in providing a sort of coarse material unity to the 'contradictory subject'. Beyond this vulgar starting point, there does seem to me to be a need to explore a historical and materialist biology, capable of examining the interconnected development of biology and social arrangements, and which does not simply surrender the category of biology to the extra-social realm of the natural where it continues to provide a fertile ground for those ideologists of the natural order of things whose contemporary incarnation is socio-biology.[3] This, I think, is a rather different project from the Foucauldian body, which since it made the transition from being rent and torn apart during the *ancien régime*, seems to have stubbornly refused to materialize. In its place, we have discourses of the body, body-politics and the micro-physics of subjecting powers. Again, I do not mean to suggest that such ideological practices are insignificant, but that their separation from the materiality of biology is strange. It requires a certain degree of security in one's body (that is an invulnerablity to starvation, physical duress and violation) to remove it to a question of discourse.

The purpose of this route through biology is to establish one of the preconditions for thinking about the material character of a – complexly – unitary subject, embodied, literally, in an individual.[4] The second precondition is to return to the analysis of individuals (subjects) who are positioned relationally as well as discursively. That is to say, a view of individuals materialized not only in bodies but also within a particular set of social relations whose main axes of division and interrelation in contemporary capitalist societies are those of class, gender and ethnicity. Within these axes of division and interrelation, and in their complex articulations, are conditions of contradiction and antagonism, exploitation and oppression. There are also the simultaneous processes of ideological signification which generate and offer (rather than directly constitute) subjectivities or identities, which play across the social or relational positioning of individuals.[5] I want to argue that it is only by considering the subject as standing at the intersection of both relational and ideological processes that it is possible to think about a subject who is, at one and the same time, unitary and contradictory: what Marx called a 'unity-in-difference'. To take the subject as solely constituted by the multiplicity of discourses–texts–interpellations is to produce a concept of the subject as plural, and eternally open to the next address which comes its way. That is to say, there are no relational lines of force which work to produce correspondences, connections or articulations with particular ideological interpellations for particular subjects or which work against articulations with other identities. As a consequence, I suspect that the postmodern concept of the subject may be formally correct, if one only considers the subject as the effect of signifying practice. Dematerialized and not relationally located, there are no grounds for thinking that such a subject is contradictory. On the contrary, the effect (the subject effect) of a plurality of discourses is a plural, or fragmentary or schizophrenic, subject. There are no analytic grounds for thinking that the relation between such plural discourses is one of antagonism or contradiction. In that sense alone, Lyotard is right in arguing that the proper designation is that of paradox or ambiguity – for there is nothing here but language games.

These relations of a social division of labour are also processes: of labour and of social practice. In the most mundane sense, subjects are interesting because they do things. A central part of what contemporary subjects do is to take part in the processes of a capitalist circuit of production – the processes of production, exchange, distribution and consumption. The specific forms of these general processes have changed, and, indeed, continue to change (the expansion of sectors not directly involved in the production of objects, for example). But they continue to be processes which are linked, which require labours and subjects to perform those labours, and which retain a recognizable organizing structure.

It is worth remarking how many theories of consumer capitalism (of which postmodernism may be one exotic variant) have come to take capitalism at its face value: as a system of circulation, exchange and consumption. In doing so, they manage to reproduce the problem of commodity fetishism: the obscuring of the conditions and relations of production. It is as if the BurgerKing I consumed while reading Lyotard did not rest on a whole system of capitalized agriculture, transportation systems, food processing plants as well as the service economy of cooking and exchange that takes place in the house of the BurgerKing itself. The 'hidden abode' of production needs to be rediscovered – not because some absolute secret will be discerned there – but simply because the rest of the processes and relations will not make sense without it. In its absence, they do, indeed, come to look arbitrary and disconnected. There is another reason to urge its rediscovery, because, in some ways, the hidden abode is now more hidden. The appearance of a consumer culture in the Western metropolitan centres – the excess of commodities and signs – rests decisively upon the transfer of production to its new abodes in the Third World.

There are further reasons for insisting upon seeing consumption as a process involving labour or practice (including signifying practice). It is all too tempting to elide these practices into a single instantaneous act of consumption, swallowing the subject into the commodity, as if this act of consumption did not require the labours of shopping and cooking or cleaning, and so forth. The consumer culture has effected a powerful reorganization of the private sphere of domestic labour: in some cases taking it into the public realm, in what Braverman (1974) called the 'universal market', while in other ways intensifying the quality and quantity of the labour needed to maintain the private realm. Only male intellectuals, one is tempted to say, could construct such an elision of the labour and act of consumption, or be capable of such conceptual amnesia.

I also want to insist that this concern with labours and practices includes the issues of ideological work or signifying practices. Only at the highest levels of abstraction is it possible to insist on a formal separation of the economic and the ideological. Concretely, they are materialized together. But I also want to claim that the work of ideology continues to be the construction of individual and collective meanings. The postmodern condition of 'in-difference' to meaning seems to me to be the result of its juxtaposition with a realm of meaning. Its indifference relies on the difference constructed between itself and meaning. It is a condition which Larry Grossberg has ironically dubbed 'pose-modernism' (1988: p. 19). Leaving this pursuit of indifference aside, ideological work continues to be the site of collective struggles to command meaning, to engage meanings in the practice of creating or sustaining collective identities, directions and projects and to exclude others. The overarching US symbolism of *e pluribus unum* has historically been the site of extensive ideological struggles to define who is included or excluded from the 'one' (native Americans, Afro-Caribbean slaves, Hispanics, women and the recurring 'Godless Communists' in their many guises). Such definitional issues continue to be a matter of political and ideological struggle, as in the legal cases surrounding the efforts of the Sanctuary Movement to aid refugees from Central America, where the test of access to becoming part of the 'one' lies in the refugees' status as political or economic refugees. At the same time, the character and project of the 'one' (the Nation itself) has also been the object of political and ideological struggles, whose outcomes are not an insignificant matter for the rest of the world.[6]

THE END OF HISTORY (PART ONE): OR, ENTER THE CYBERNAUTS

Standing at the edge of time, with nowhere much to go, one is left with idle thoughts which turn (Lyotard-like) to matters of paradox. One such is that while History has stopped, the world has continued to turn. I am confronted by visions of postmodernists as our contemporary King Canutes – testing Divine Providence by attempting to stop the flow of the tide. Where King Canute got his feet wet when the tide prevailed, my hope is that when the tide next ebbs, our contemporaries will be left high and dry: flotsam-like, their only function will be to interrupt the beach. Such language games as these are occasioned by a peculiar conflation which has taken place in the province of history in the world of critical theory. It is a conflation of History with history. The vanquished Subject of History might well have been a fantastic, metaphysical ideo-logical figment–figleaf: a teleological, ontological, essentialist, speculative, Hegelian conception of the uni-linear development of the idea, God, progress or the revolutionary working class, and *its* passing should cause us to shed few tears. But concepts should not be conflated with their objects (unless we are willing to take the leap of faith and claim there are no objects). Only philosophers, one might say, could mistake slaying the idea (History) for stopping real movement through time (history).

Something in the rhetorical excess, the signifying richness, of the assault on History in postmodernist texts suggests a certain nervousness. The surplus of signs which are used to fix the end of History, the many theoretical stakes which are driven through the heart of the vampire-subject, suggest that these processes may come back to haunt us. This excess of signs works to conceal the conflation of History and history, and leaves unresolved the problem of what to do with history if History is dead. Instead, I think we might celebrate the end of History in a more archaic fashion: History is dead, long live history: neither law-like in its progression, nor absolutely lawless; neither absolutely determined nor absolutely indeterminate. From such a starting point, it is possible to join in one of the celebrations of postmodernism: the jettisoning of false philosophical dualisms, and to add one more to the list of things to go. While freely dispensing with those old philosophical inheritances of empiricism and metaphysics, let us also shed the one which lurks at the heart of postmodernism – the Absolute or the Void.

However, how we got to the Void (or its fragmentary equivalent) is, as they used to say, another story. One of the recurrent concerns of recent critical theorizing, and a central theme in postmodernism, is the assault on the error strewn totalizing systems of past intellectual practice. But in the processes of deconstruction, the postmodernists have (as intellectuals are wont to do) reconstructed a new system, a new totality. The postmodern condition rests upon the model (the simulacrum) of cybernetic systems theory. The postmodernists have discovered the info-tech future, and it works (if it's plugged in).

It is this adoption of a cybernetic model which accounts for the abolition of time (the instants of instantaneous communication), as though no-one made the key strokes. It accounts for the disconnection of signs and meaning (the 'bits' of knowledge), as though there were no processes of progamming and encoding. It is this model which constantly underpins the observations about the postmodern condition: from Baudrillard's discussion of the collapse of public and private realms, through the concern with the immediacy and transparent effectivity of the 'flickers' of reality, to Lyotard's interest in 'communicative instability' and 'negative feedback loops'. The analyses of postmodernism constantly both refer to the expansion of information technology as a feature of the contemporary world, and use the cybernetic model it embodies to explain the contemporary condition.

There is, of course, no wonder that this model works so well for the postmodernist: it functions so smoothly precisely because it is a model of a unitary system from which all concepts of contradiction or antagonism have been expelled. Long ago, before the cybernetic version of it became embedded in the new information technology, varieties of systems theory were subjected to extensive critiques precisely because of their organic presumptions. They were incapable of grasping that a system could exist which, in place of functional and organic connections, contained disjunctures, contradictions and conflict: a system whose 'harmony' is, as Althusser put it, 'teeth-gritting'. For the postmodernists, there are no 'bugs in the system', because a systemic model has been adopted which has no place for bugs. One of the saddest passages in postmodernist writing appears at the end of Lyotard's *The Postmodern Condition*, where he 'remembers' that there are different possible futures. One is that the new information technology could become the 'dream instrument for controlling and regulating the market system'; the other is that:

> it could also aid groups discussing metaprescriptives by supplying them with the information they usually lack for making knowledgeable decisions. The line to follow for computerization to take the second of these two paths is, in principle, quite simple: give the public free access to the memory and data banks . . . This sketches the outline of a politics that would respect the desire for justice and the desire for the unknown. (1984: 67.)

I find this passage sad because, as Frederic Jameson points out in his Introduction to the book, it rests on a 'narrative' (Justice), whose preconditions have been systematically deconstructed in the preceding 66 pages. It also summons up an impossible collective Subject (The Public) which postmodernism has already consigned to the dustbin of history. Lyotard's 'sketch', then, is merely gestural. At the end of History, there are no material grounds to sustain such a politics.

All of this, including the pathos of Lyotard's gesture, proceeds from the systemic model, when, viewed from history, it might have looked rather different. From within the model, it is possible to forget the struggles which have taken place over the politics of data control and access; to forget the struggles over the introduction and use of new technology; to forget the struggles which take place at the chip-producing and assembling ends of the imperial communicating chain. Such forgetting is possible because amnesia is another key element of the postmodern condition. Having consigned such stories to the past ('we', says Lyotard, 'no longer have nostalgia for such narratives'), he has, indeed, nowhere to go.

Where Lyotard sees us as being beyond narratives, and even beyond nostalgia for them, Baudrillard takes a more cautious view of how fully developed the postmodern condition is. He has noticed that not all of us have either found or lost our feet in the postmodern world, observing that 'all of this does not mean that the domestic universe . . . is still not lived largely in a traditional way . . . It means rather that the stakes are no longer there, that another arrangement or lifestyle is virtually in place.' (1983: 133.) For those of us who have not yet received the invitation to step beyond history, some of these traditional ways linger on, and not only in the domestic sphere. For us – the masses – the postmodernists appear to have nothing but the massive contempt which the avant-garde always shows to those who have failed to catch up with the new 'lifestyle'.

For many people, and in many different ways, the 'narratives' of history and politics have not gone away. To be living (however briefly) in a USA where the reign of Reagan saw the Dow-Jones Index boom and where nine million new 'poor subjects' (living below the official poverty line) have been created, is to experience something of the contradictory process of history. To have lived – first in Britain and then in the USA – through a time of military adventures in the South Atlantic, Grenada, Nicaragua and Libya, is to feel the weight of 'national narratives' which stubbornly refuse to die (although they kill others on their way). And these narratives are not, as Frederic Jameson has argued (1984: xii), repressed or in the unconscious, they are open, overt and unashamed. Lest these be taken as depressing thoughts, from which an escape into the hyper-reality of postmodernism suddenly begins to look attractive, it is important to remember that there are other (still subordinate) narratives which resist both the existing forms of economic and political domination, and the proclaimed end of History. In the struggles of people as workers, citizens, feminists, people of colour, and, perhaps most of all in the struggles of people in the Third World to construct new possibilities of national sovereignty, democracy and social-ism, there are new political narratives being constructed which are more than fragments if less than History. In 1963, Edward

Thompson remarked on the historian's obligation to rescue the
stories of the emergent English working class from the 'massive
condescension of history'. In the postmodern age, there is now a
double obligation: to valorize such stories against the condescension of history and against the amnesia of the end of History.

NAMING THE ENEMY:
OR, WHOSE IMPLOSION IS THIS?

In his book *Towards 2000*, Raymond Williams reflects upon an
earlier process of technological, cultural and political transformation in analysing how modernism in aesthetic and cultural
practice became absorbed and normalized. His observations provide a useful starting point for thinking about postmodernism.

What was eventually projected as the 'global village' of modern communications was the fantastic projection of a few centres which had reduced human content to its simplest univer-
sally transmissible forms . . . Thus the very conditions which
had provoked a genuine modernist art became the conditions
which steadily homogenised even its startling images . . .
  The two faces of this 'modernism' could literally not recognise each other, until a very late stage. Their uneasy relationship was interpreted by a displacement. On the one hand
what was seen as the energetic minority art of a time of
reduction and dislocation; on the other hand the routines
of a technologised 'mass' culture . . . .
  The dominance of a few centres of 'universal' production,
and the simultaneous dominance of artistic and intellectual
life by a few metropolitan centres, have now to be seen as
inherently related. The climax of the pretensions by which
this situation was hidden was the widely accepted proposition
of the 'global village'. What was being addressed was a real
development of universal distribution and unprecedented
opportunities for genuine and diverse cultural exchange. What
was ideologically inserted was a model of an homogenised
humanity consciously served from two or three centres:
the monopolising corporations and the elite metropolitan
intellectuals. *One practised the homogenisation, the other*

theorised it. Each found its false ground in the technologies which had 'changed and opened up the world and brought it together'. But nothing in the technologies led to this theory or practice. The real forces which produced both, not only in culture but in the widest areas of social, economic and political life, belonged to the dominant capitalist order in its paranational phase. *But this was an enemy which could not be named because its money was being taken.* (1983: 142–3, emphasis added.)

These observations, and especially Williams' characteristically lucid rejection of the 'technological fix', provide a starting point for thinking about differences between modernism and 'postmodernism'. For me, one of the most striking differences is that where Williams argues that 'the two faces of modernism could not recognise one another', the two faces of postmodernism (one, the new communicative technologies; the other, the intellectual practices of postmodernism) have recognized one another immediately. It is a love-at-first-sight affair: an implosion of postmodernist intellectuals into the new technology. Where modernism had to make a historical transition from its original intention to outrage bourgeois sentiment to its capitalized absorption into a 'universal' culture, postmodernism celebrates its immediate fit. No longer a source of outrage, merely another form of enrichment. Postmodernism has learned to love the enemy which 'could not be named' and the result is 'ecstasy'. Even so, naming the enemy still proves to be difficult because the ideology of technology remains the link through which this affair of the head (rather than the heart) is consummated. The name still refuses to come to the lips – or appear on the VDU – so we are left in hyper-reality . . .

But in order to do more than describe, it is necessary to think about the conditions that have changed the 'two faces' in the contemporary world: the face of technology and the face of the metropolitan intellectuals. For the former, we need to address the complex conditions of the whole process of capitalist 'speed up' through the 1970s and 80s. Some of its forms are all too familiar: the continuing speed up of production lines; the increasing velocity of capital as it moves hither and thither across the globe in search of new sources of cheap labour and good business climates; and the growing rapaciousness of finance capital as it guts existing enterprises in the search for fast profits.[7] At the same time, though, 'speed up' has dominated the processes of distribution, exchange and, of necessity, since surplus value must still be realized, consumption itself. The reorganization of systems of transportation, business communication, the expansion and simultaneous computerization of credit, the multiplication of forms and points of consumption in the metropolitan countries – all of these are marked by increasing velocity, and their reorganization has relied on the integration of the new technologies. The continued expansion of a system of production needs a commensurate expansion of consumption (in which is embedded the signifying richness of the USA as a consumer society). I do not mean to suggest that these changes have taken place in any simple or functional progression, for they have not. Many of the developments took place precisely to overcome blockages or contradictions in the existing performance of the system: the intractability of particular labour forces; the financial costs of welfare states; the regulations imposed upon processes of capital accumulation; the problems of coordinating processes of production, distribution and exchange over space and through time, which exist as barriers to be overcome, not abolished.[8]

This is not to reduce the development and integration of new technologies to some abstract logic of capital, but nor are they mere accidents. Their development and articulation with existing processes of production, exchange, distribution and consumption has rested upon the prevailing conditions, on strategic decisions and on conflicts about their deployment. They are enmeshed in, not separate from, the complex of economic, cultural and political struggles. Nor does their introduction herald an end to those struggles. They do not mark the dawn of a new, conflict-free, era. They rearrange how and where those struggles are to take place; they affect the balance of forces within them, and they change the strategies which can be employed in them, but they do not abolish them.

There is no doubt that one of the central areas in which these reorganizations have taken place is that of communications. Some of these changes have had their impact upon labour processes (new technologies provide more efficient means of command and coordination). Some have had their effects on the realms of exchange and circulation (aiding the range and velocity of capital); and some are felt in the arena of consumption (satellite and cable as new means of access to the home). And, not surprisingly since so many of the new technologies are information technologies, their impact has been felt in the systems of cultural production, distribution and consumption. One aspect of the process of speed up has been the increasing valorization of signs: the multiplication of communicative texts as commodities. What remains striking about this process (for all the postmodern conceptions of arbitrariness, indifference and fragmentation) is how narrow the range of meanings has remained in the dominant media of communication. The range, as well as the internal articulation, of mediated meanings, remains an object of political and cultural struggle, in addition to being an object of economic power. The 'Many' of America continue to be represented through such mediated cultural signs, for example, the 'body count' of *Miami Vice* contains a strikingly high proportion of Hispanics, and its heroes are more than coincidentally male; while Stallone embodies (literally and metaphorically) a distinctive version of what the 'One' of America is about.[9] While changes in technology may have brought us closer to the terminal, it is also important to remember that what appears on the screen does not exhaust the world. It is the product of one set of cultural and economic institutions which articulates with other cultural practices through subjects who are embedded in social processes, and engaged in their own signifying practices.

There remains the question as to what has changed in the other 'face' of Williams' formulation: that of the élite metropolitan intellectuals; and here my answer will be rather briefer. That face, especially in its postmodern guise, looks like the consequence of a process of multiple marginalizations, whose layers can be quickly traced. First, there is the marginalization of metropolitan intellectuals in the process of global economic and political reorganization (where the focal points have moved towards the Third World). Secondly, there is the continuing marginalization of European metropolitan intellectuals under the economic, political and cultural hegemony of the USA.

Thirdly, there is the national-popular marginalization of the intellectuals in terms of our domestic political effectivity (the failure of the revolutionary subject to materialize in response to our summons). Fourthly, there is the marginalization of male intellectuals by the rise and vitality of feminism as a political and cultural force. From these multiple and over-determined marginalizations, it is possible to think about who is at the end of History, and how they got there. In one sense, the long march of the Western intellectuals through the theories of the superstructure may have ended here – in postmodernism and the celebration of the end of everything. But if we take a view of these postmodern intellectuals as having arrived *outside* history, rather than at its funeral, then it may be easier to find our way back to the pressing problems of understanding the interdependent processes of chaos and order which Dick Hebdige has eloquently described as 'the bottom line on Planet One' (1985). In the terms in which I have been arguing here, that is a return to the task of thinking about a system which contains contradictions, antagonisms and struggles; about lives in which subjects do more than watch TV; and about forms of social organization which are 'unities in difference': *e pluribus unum*, indeed.

A POSTSCRIPT ON POSTCARDS

There is one final thought – to speed us on our different ways. For theorists who are committed to the end of narrative, to the untotalizable character of existence, and to the fragmentation of the subject, the postmodernists remain strikingly fond of telling us stories about who, where and when we are. Their characteristic mode of address is 'we': we are here; we feel this; we no longer want that, and so on. It is, of course, another totalizing 'we' that is being deployed: an interpellation of 'us' in another narrative. If the postmodernists have indeed gone beyond history and have arrived in the fragmented universe of no-when and no-where, I merely wish that they would stop sending postcards back to the rest of us which are emblazoned with the eternal postcard message: 'Wish you were here'.

NOTES

This chapter was developed through a series of seminars while I was visiting the Department of Curriculum and Instruction at the University of Wisconsin-Madison, and I am grateful to those who took part for encouraging me to think. My thoughts have also been much helped by conversations with Larry Grossberg, Allen Hunter, Mike Apple and Leslie Roman. It was originally published in a special issue of *Communication* (1988, Vol. 10) devoted to a discussion of postmodernism.

1   The fact that such 'witches' are occasional might be thought to identify the conjunction of two processes in theorizing. One is the inflationary spiral of theorizing-as-academic-capital; the other is the use of such capital in reconstructing male preserves in the face of feminist incursions (as the author's own gender indicates).

2   This paradox is manifested in a different way in the splitting of the critical academic world between those who study texts and discourses (the disciplines of literary theory, communications, film studies, and so on) and those who study social relations and economic processes (sociology, economics, and so forth). Apparently the two don't get to meet much – not even sitting next to one another on the shelves in the bookshop.

3   By proceeding via this pincer attack – the dual condemnation of empiricism and metaphysics – the 'discursive constitution of everything' position attempts to exclude the possibility of non-empiricist realist epistemologies. Not being an epistemologist, I must leave this matter to others ... and proceed as if there is.

4   Such approaches are being worked on by biologists, who appear on still further distant shelves in the bookshops. See, for example, Lewontin, Rose and Kamin 1984, and Birke 1986.

5   I am conscious that my language here is replete with back-sliding, pre-scientific words and phrases, such as individuals, identities and labours. This is, in part, because I am no longer convinced that the rites of theoretical ppppppurification should require that words are purged because they are tainted, thus necessitating their replacement with new (and often longer) ones. So, for anyone who cares, when I use the word 'individual', I do not mean the individual of bourgeois ideology; when I use the word iddeeennntttity it contains no presumption that an individual has only one; and when I use the word 'labour' I mean more than the narrow connotation of male manual labour in factory production. Signs are polysemic . . . .

6   Alan Trachtenberg's *The Incorporation of America* (1982) offers a fascinating account and analysis of some of the struggles over the meaning of America.

7   Some of these processes, their economic and political conditions,
    and their social effects, are analysed in Bluestone and Harrison
    (1983).
8   There is a particularly interesting, if not very attractive, coincidence
    between Baudrillard's remarks on the redundancy of 'the immense
    geographical countryside' and the current economic and social cri-
    sis in American farming. As usual, I think it is a coincidence which
    requires a materialist explanation (Baudrillard 1983: 129).
9   I do not mean to suggest that such crude observations exhaust
    the problems of ideological or textual analysis. However, being
    significations, perhaps they have some significance.

3

The American way: processes of class and cultural formation

If the problems of postmodernism can be traced, in part, to the inflation of the importance of the symbolic order at the expense of the material, then it is surely possible to look to Marxism – the theory which has given pre-eminence to the materiality of social relations – to redress the balance. Contemporary Marxism, however, does not exactly offer a trouble-free zone in which to pursue such answers. There is no uni-vocal orthodoxy from which an analysis of the present can be drawn. If anything, contemporary Marxism contains more varieties than Heinz ever dreamt of. Some of this diversity stems from the revival, in the 1970s, of interest in Marxism as a social theory which multiplied efforts to revive and update classical Marxism. But it also results from the problems of analysing late twentieth century capitalism, while still holding to the basic propositions of Marxist theory. One site of these difficulties is the 'problem of the middle-classes': that troubling, and expanding, lump of the population that fails to correspond to either of the great class positions of capitalism: bourgeois or proletariat. The middle classes pose an empirical threat to the theoretical tidiness of Marxism, and their presence also raises troubling questions about their political, ideological and cultural effects on class relations. There is also the equally pressing problem of how to deal with what, in conventional terms, can be termed the non-economic elements of contemporary society: the superstructures of ideology, consciousness, culture and politics. Finally, Marxism has struggled to come to terms with the salience, and political effectivity, of gender and race as patterns of social differentiation. All of these have been the object of some tortured and tortuous rethinking among Marxist scholars, anxious both to demonstrate the superior analytic power of Marxism over competing theories and to retain the purity of classical Marxist concepts.

In this chapter, I want to explore some of the limitations of reformulations of political economy orthodoxy in the face of the non-economic (or cultural) processes of class formation and to consider an alternative which aims to avoid either marginalizing such cultural processes or surrendering them to non-Marxist forms of inquiry. I shall be pursuing these arguments with reference to examples from processes of class formation in the USA. This choice is not a casual one: the USA represents the most advanced case for both Marxist and non-Marxist accounts of social relations. On the one hand, as the leading capitalist economy, it is a society where orthodox political economy ought to find considerable analytical leverage. On the other, its peculiarities, particularly of race and ethnicity, have provided a fertile ground for the advancement of theories stressing cultural pluralism or a politics of difference. As a result, the nature of American class formation has long exercised a distinctive fascination.

THE WRIGHT STUFF:
STUDYING CLASS FORMATION

One way of restating the problem of class analysis is to refer to the movement from the abstract concept of the capitalist mode of production to studying the way capitalism works in specific societies. This separates the abstraction of the mode of production with its delineation of the essential class positions in the social relations of production (the owners and non-owners of the means of production), from the rich complexity of social relations which are embodied in a particular society. Confronting the analyst at this point is not only the empirical messiness of class formations (the middle classes especially), but also the diversity of other social relations – in particular those of race and gender.

Although the problems of moving from the abstract to the concrete in studying class formations have received extensive consideration, I want to concentrate here on one of the most developed and systematic attempts to reformulate Marxist political economy for the study of specific class formations: the work of Erik Olin Wright, in his book *Classes* (1985). Wright's arguments highlight some of the problems which I want to use here as a basis for developing an alternative way of thinking about class and culture.

Wright (1985: 109) argues that in moving from the abstract to the concrete, it is important to distinguish three levels of analysis. First is the mode of production, the most abstract form of analysis in which the basic structure of, capitalism in this case, is laid bare. The second is the level of 'social formations', and the third is the study of 'conjunctures' – the concrete patterns of particular societies at specific historical moments. In moving from the mode of production to the study of social formations one encounters societies which are composed of more than one mode of production articulated together. Thus, while capitalist social formations may be characterized by the dominance of the capitalist mode of production and its structure of class relations, this will be articulated with elements of other residual or emergent modes of production (feudal, slave or socialist) which will add divergent forms of class structure to the elementary forms of capitalist relations.

This combination of modes of production provides the basis for Wright's account of the middle classes (beyond the traditional *petit bourgeoisie*). He is concerned to develop a coherent analysis based on the essential Marxist concept of 'exploitation' – which he argues his own earlier conception of the middle classes being the product of 'contradictory class locations' failed to do. He now argues that the capitalist mode of production (and its mode of exploitation of wage labour) needs to be seen as being combined with two other modes of exploitation. These are 'statism', which rests on the exploitation of organization assets; and 'socialism' which is based upon the exploitation of 'skill/credential assets' (1985: 76–82). These modes of exploitation, he argues, give rise to distinct class positions in social formations dominated by the capitalist mode of production.

I will return to these arguments later in the chapter, but for the moment I want to concentrate on Wright's approach to the connection between class and other social relations. In *Classes*, he argues that the consideration of non-class elements of social relations – race and gender, in particular – need to be added to the analysis of class relations. The problem he faces is where to include them: in which of the levels of analysis are they to be integrated? Wright settles for their inclusion at the conjunctural level, the most concrete. This is primarily on the grounds that neither race nor gender have been adequately theorized at the level of the mode of production (1985: 11–12). While this may represent a step forward in relation to some Marxist positions which treat them as entirely extraneous, Wright's route nevertheless leaves them in a relatively peripheral situation. Non-class elements make their appearance at the moment of conjunctural analysis (the study of specific historical moments), where their effectivity can be assessed in terms of their consequences for the primary concerns with class formation.

This results in a travesty of an inclusion of race and gender which manages to both overestimate and underestimate the importance of class analysis. It overestimates by presuming a pre-existing class of wage labourers with a class consciousness which is then somehow affected by historically contingent factors. No such class does – or could – exist. It implies the presence of a class of ungendered and unraced labourers who are here and there interrupted by becoming gendered and raced. Such a view of class consciousness and class membership is an impossibility because the members of a class will always be historically contingent: formed in the full complexity of the social relations of their society. In this way, Wright's work continues to reproduce the worst problems of class essentialism by claiming an unfounded primacy for class membership over the marginalized contingencies of other social positions and identities. Wright's argument rests on an elision between the centrality of class relations in the mode of production, and their place in a particular society. Its effects on his analysis can be seen in his empirical comparison of class consciousness in the USA and Sweden. The differences between the two are partially explained by reference to historically contingent political and ideological factors, such as levels of unionization and forms of political discourse, which are themselves unexamined because of the primacy attributed to class structure (1985: 278–280).

I also want to argue here that Wright's formulation of class versus non-class elements underestimates the importance of class analysis. This distinction leaves race and gender as free floating relations separated from the realm of class and suffers from the reverse of the problem about an ungendered and unraced class. If the labourer is always materialized with a specific racial and gendered character in a social formation, then the obverse point must be made. Neither race nor gender stand 'naked' outside of class relations. These different social relations materialize together – they are condensed in the formation of each social subject. This is not to say that there are not different principles at stake in these relations (patriarchy and racism, for example), but that these – like the abstract distinction between bourgeois and proletariat – should not be conflated with the concrete complexity of their combination in a particular society.

The articulation of these different axes of social relations is all too briefly remarked upon in Wright's study, in spite of his own data revealing that over 60 per cent of the working class in the USA is female and over 75 per cent is black. It seems difficult to accept that such profound racial and gender structuring of class membership can be the result of mere historical contingency. Rather, it suggests that it is impossible to think about the processes of class formation in the USA without looking at the intersection of gender and racial structuring. At the abstract level of the capitalist mode of production, it may be true that the constituent classes of capitalism may be gender and race blind concepts, but the same cannot, and should not, be claimed for classes in the societies in which that mode of production is materialized. It is in this sense that I think Wright does a disservice to class analysis by his marginalization of race and gender, leaving them as untheorized elements outside of class relations. All social subjects, including the reserve army of labour (who, for some reason, are left out of Wright's class analysis) are 'bathed in the glow' of capitalist social relations. Within a capitalist social formation there is no hiding place. Indeed, had Wright ventured to include the unemployed – the non-working fraction of the proletariat – the already extensive proletarianization of women and black males would have been that much more intensified.

What this highlights is a problem with Wright's separation of the three levels of analysis. I shall have more to say about the mode of production later, but here I want to comment on the levels of the 'social formation' and the 'conjuncture'. For Wright, social formations are the combination of modes of production: a stepping-stone to the analysis of concrete societies whose class formation is shaped by multiple modes of production. However, it is not clear what extra analytic advantage he gains by limiting the concept of the social formation to such a combination. I think it is more productive to use the concept to refer to the materialization of such multiple modes of production in a specific society, together with all those elements sometimes referred to, rather passively, as the 'conditions of existence' of a mode of production. Here one would include all those superstructural elements of political, juridical, social and cultural processes in which a mode of production is realized. Such a concept is more historically and societally specific than that proposed by Wright, which operates merely as a shadow concept of the mode of production. A more expansive view of the social formation fills the otherwise excessive analytical gap that opens up between Wright's 'social formation' and the 'conjuncture'.

If we accept Wright's view of 'conjuncture' as referring to a specific society at a particular historical moment, then 'contingencies' affecting class formation cannot be analysed without an intervening level between them and modes of production. A more concrete view of social formations (as referring, for example, to late twentieth century USA, or pre-Civil War America) allows the exploration of the formative impact of non-economic processes on class formations. Such factors as levels of unionization or forms of political discourse can be seen as the consequences of previous conjunctures on the social formation: the sedimented accretions of the history of a social formation. In these terms, conjunctures are of interest not as a synchronic snapshot of a society at a particular moment, but because of their impacts on the organic development of that society: their modifications or exacerbations of its dominant tendencies. Wright's limited conception of 'social formation' allows no space for such historical or diachronic concerns, with the effect that history can only be a series of non-integrated conjunctures.[1]

The result of Wright's formulation is the *ad hoc* listing of factors (political discourse, form of the state, etc.) which have no structured location. A more expanded view of the social formation also allows the location of formations of race and gender and their intersection with class, even if concepts for their analysis cannot be theorized at the level of the mode of production. It should be said that this hardly counts as a strike against them, since there are many Marxist concepts that cannot be elaborated at this level of abstraction.

'WHAT EVERY CHILD KNOWS': THE CIRCUITS OF CAPITAL

In trying to construct an alternative to such essentialist views of class formation, I want to begin from where almost everyone else finds the starting point – the analysis of the capitalist mode of production in Marx's *Capital*. I will not linger too long over the assertion that (as almost everybody agrees) classes in Marx's analysis are relational: that is, they are based in social relations of production that create the appropriation of surplus value by the class which possesses a particular form of property – capital – from a class which is obliged to sell its labour power. But *Capital* delivers considerably more than that bare outline. Most significantly, it analyses the way in which those relations are embodied in a process through which surplus value is both produced and accumulated. The capitalist mode of production involves the 'circuit of capital': the processes of production, circulation, exchange and consumption. *Capital* describes the workings of this circuit (the 'laws of motion' of capitalism) and what Marx stresses, even at this level of abstraction, is that the completion of this circuit (the accumulation of surplus value) is a profoundly messy and complicated process. The 'laws of motion', although we might, in this less positivist age, call them tendencies so as not to offend tender philosophical consciences, are not simple and straightforward, but include gaps, interruptions, blockages, tensions and contradictions, which need to be overcome before the circuit can be completed and the process can begin again. What *Capital* provides us with is an analysis of the capitalist mode of production as relational, processual and problematic. I have stressed these words because the influence of structuralism on Marxist analysis since the 1970s has had the effect of reducing the capitalist mode of production to a formalized architecture of positions which omits precisely these processual and problematic qualities of Marx's analysis.

Even at this abstract level, one can identify some of the generic problems which characterize the capitalist mode of production: the inhibitions which capital must seek to overcome to complete its circuit profitably. One is that capital is not a general entity, but a particularized one: a multiplicity of capitals whose relationship is one of competition over the possible sources of profitability. Competition is both a generic feature of the process, and (from the standpoint of any particular capital) an inhibition to maximum profitability. Secondly, the relationship between labour and capital is both inter-dependent and antagonistic, since labour power must be paid less than the value it creates in order to generate surplus value. The wage is thus a structural point of conflict. Thirdly, for surplus value to be realized (turned into profit) commodities must be sold. They must get to a market and find a buyer able to pay the price. As a consequence, a variety of problems are embedded in the process of realization: transport, the organization of exchange, the availability of purchasing power, and so forth.

These remarks are relatively banal: they are (as Marx was fond of saying) 'what every child knows' about the workings of capitalism. They are still worth remembering however, because they are not some extraneous adjunct to the capitalist mode of production but are intrinsic to its processes. They are significant because they point to the dynamic sense which Marx gives to capitalism: they are the potential blockages which capital must strive to overcome. Capitalists must aim to coordinate the processes of the circuit of capital to ensure that surplus value is both produced and realized. Coordination is an integral issue in the capitalist mode of production precisely because the processes of capital accumulation are inherently problematic.

Such a view of the mode of production, and the importance of coordination within it, provides one starting point for thinking about the problem of the middle classes. Coordination requires coordinators. But at this level of abstraction, there is not a lot more to be said, since how coordination takes place – and who performs such tasks – are matters which need to be analysed in their proper place: in terms of class formation. The particular forms of coordination (market researchers, line managers, budgetary controllers, and so on) cannot be divined from an abstract analysis of the circuit of capital any more than can the particular forms which wage labour takes (shoe-making, milling, painting, and so forth).

There is one final point to be made before leaving this abstracted world of the mode of production. An emphasis on seeing the relations and processes which constitute it as antagonistic and problematic might help to avoid some of the problems associated with theories which have analysed the reproduction of capitalism, and examined the contribution which different agencies and institutions (from the welfare state to the family) make to such reproduction. All too often, such theories have turned out to have a distinctly functionalist cast, not least because they have viewed the object being reproduced (the social relations of capitalism) as a system which is only formally contradictory, rather than as a set of inherently problematic processes. It would be preferable to see reproduction as the attempt to coordinate both a set of relationships and a set of processes which are unstable. Such a view would highlight the work that has to be done to secure their reproduction, as well as registering that the outcome of reproduction is the continued existence of an unstable system.

FURTHER PARTICULARS:
THE HISTORICAL CONTINGENCY OF
CLASS FORMATION

I have argued that Wright's concept of the social formation was both too limited in its scope and too ahistorical to play an adequate role in the analysis of class formation. Instead I suggested that it needed to refer to the materialization of modes of production within the complex of conditions which make up a particular society. Consequently, the movement in the focus of analysis is from the abstract laws of motion of capital to the particular forms of capital and labour, embodied in the peculiarities of space, time, social, cultural and political conditions of a specific society.

Thus materialized, the processes of capital accumulation do not stand outside the society (as some separately identifiable economic base) but are embedded within it. The peculiarities of a particular society constitute not only the conditions of existence of the circuit of capital but also shape the nature of that circuit and constitute some of the potential blockages which capital must overcome (for example, the development of US capitalism has had to overcome the sheer geographical size of North America and the problems which this has posed for the coordination of distribution and communication). The economy must draw its labour from particular social actors, already formed in other social, political and cultural relations and practices. The proletariat – the class of wage labourers – has to be both formed (stripped of the means of subsistence to ensure their dependence on the wage) and recruited into particular economic positions or occupations. Analytically, the proletariat is not a natural 'given': an essence waiting to be topped up with other non-class bits and pieces. In studying this social formation, the labourer is already the American labourer, the black labourer, the female labourer and much more besides.

For the moment, though, I want to concentrate on the historical contingency of class formation itself, beginning with the relationship between labour and capital. One starting point is to return to my earlier comment about Capital being a multiplicity of particular capitals. The class of wage-labourers encounters and confonts capital in these particular forms, and not capital-in-general. Wage labour is thus a double condition: both general,in the sense of being available for hire, and particular, being formed in a relationship with a specific employer who purchases the labour and puts it to work. In such a process, labour is particularized in a variety of ways. Each labourer represents a specific configuration of skills and capacities. Labour also tends to be particularized by place. The social formation of labour in the USA, as elsewhere, has been shaped in and through communities and localities in which were embedded both a pattern of specific capitalist enterprises and localized ethnic and gender compositions of labour.[2]

Labour is also subject to a constant process of remaking. Classes are not simply formed in their moment of origin. In this section, I will be considering some aspects of this remaking viewed one-sidedly, so to speak, from the vantage point of labour processes within capitalism. Subsequently, I will look at the ways in which these remaking processes intersect with others. Braverman's analysis of 'Taylorism' (1974) highlights some of the ways in which class formation was remade during the early twentieth century – in particular, the deliberate fragmentation of labour skills to both enhance managerial control and diminish sites of resistance within labour. Gramsci's discussion of 'Fordism' (1971) points to the intersection of new forms of labour process with a range of non-economic processes of remaking and rationalization of the city and the family. In particular, he emphasizes the way new methods of production and the 'high wage economy' have been coupled with greater supervision of, and intervention into, the private life of workers in an attempt to create the new 'collective worker' (1971: 302).

In such processes, what we see are the strategies developed by capital in an effort to increase productivity and improve coordination by overcoming the blockage represented by earlier forms of working-class organization (the monopolization of skills, informal work control, and so on). Such changes also have consequences for other aspects of class formation. They may change the places of class formation, as in the major relocation of industrial production during the Second World War or in the contemporary migration of capital from the 'frostbelt' to the 'sunbelt' and the Pacific rim. They also involve changes in the social and cultural formations of class. De-skilling, capital migration and labour process reorganization do not work on existing members of the labour force alone, but are often combined with the recruitment of new sources of labour. Characteristically, such processes have attempted to undo the control of both the recruitment and the labour process exercised by white male workers in order to recruit female and ethnic labour forces. The Second World War saw a massive expansion in black and female employment, while the wave of plant closures and relocations through the 1970s and 80s has contained a drive to discover new groups of 'inexperienced' workers, within and outside the USA (Bluestone and Harrison 1982). These processes of remaking are both uneven and contradictory: Lipsitz's discussion of the recruitment of new labour during the Second World War (1982) demonstrates how the increased entry of black workers both heightened inter-racial conflict and forged black workers into collective militancy, in union activism and demands for equal treatment (for example the threatened post-war draft refusal unless government work included non-discriminatory employment conditions). The end of the War also saw a different type of remaking as employers and unions attempted to restore traditional recruitment patterns, though this alliance was itself fraught because employers tried to use the evidence of wartime 'dilution' of skill to change previous working conditions and practices (Lipsitz 1982; Tobias and Anderson 1982).

The more recent recomposition in the 1970s and 80s of American capital in search of increased profitability has brought equally far-reaching changes in class formation. The major shifts in the structure of capital (deindustrialization; growth of high-tech industries; service sector expansion and the increased volatility of capital) have been accompanied by a major remaking of class: de-unionization of the core sectors; the imposition of flexible contracts of employment; the recruitment of 'green' labour, especially in non-union states; the 're-skilling' of technical and scientific labour and the de-skilling of both blue-collar and white-collar work, and the growth of the 'reserve army' of the unemployed combined with a diminution of its welfare support (Bluestone and Harrison 1982; Davis 1986; Piven and Cloward 1982).

I want to draw two general conclusions about these processes. The first is that, even from the narrow viewpoint of economic processes of class formation, class cannot be treated as a stable entity. Both capital and labour are constantly being recomposed. The relationship is a dynamic one, affecting the particular social character of the working class in the process. There is no essential character to which contingent elements are added. In studying any specific society, the formation of class is itself historically contingent. Second, it is important to insist that such remakings of class formation, though often driven by the innovations of capital, cannot be viewed as the accomplishments of capital against a passive working class. Such a sanguine view of capital's success cannot be sustained in the face of the continual ferment of innovation which capital is obliged to engage in to find new ways through the blockages which labour represents. Taylorism, assembly lines, automation, semi-autonomous work groups, the high wage economy, banning or breaking union organization, discriminatory hiring practices, capital migration and industrial relocation, 'human relations' management and the rest, provide a long historical testimony to the difficulty of subjugating labour. All of this, of course, needs to be understood in terms of the continuously reproduced capacity of labour to be intractable. Such resistance is not a direct class consciousness: its forms reflect the complexities of class formation. They are often limited, particular, fragmented, contradictory and frequently regressive in broader political terms (how many heroic struggles also need also to be seen as the defence of exclusive white and male privileges?). But any analysis of capitalist development that forgets the minutiae of such resistances – the overall sheer bloody-mindedness of labour – is destined to be an analysis in which the working class are the passive victims of 'reproduction'.

GIFT HORSES AND TROJAN HORSES: THE CULTURAL FORMATION OF CLASSES

It is now widely agreed that such forms of social division as gender and race cannot simply be read off as the inventions of capitalism ('let's divide the working class . . . good idea, what shall we use?'). But neither does capitalism leave them untouched as exogenous and eternally fixed qualities which, every now and then, intersect with class relations. At one level, pre-existent forms of social division must be counted as 'free gifts' to capital, inherited from previous modes of production and their social formations. But capitalism also puts these divisions to work – both literally and metaphorically – transforming them in the process. The shape of the development of US capitalism was profoundly affected by the colonial relations with native Americans. Trachtenberg (1982) describes how capitalist expansionism elaborated a distinctive set of legal and cultural relations between 'civilization' and 'savagery' whose internal logic – domestic dependent nations, tutelage, the establishment of economic rights and their military enforcement – uncomfortably prefigured the USA's subsequent logic of external imperialism. The other colonial relation, that of the Slave Trade, had an equally profound effect on the formation of US capitalism, both fuelling its early development, and subsequently acting as a fetter to its industrializing expansion.

Both of these sets of relations highlight the dangers of functionalist formulations of the relation between capitalism and race which would stress the advantages accruing to capital from the existence of such divisions, focusing on the fact that capital does 'put them to work'. Such formulations are flawed in a variety of ways. Most importantly, they miss the effort that is expended on making such divisions productive: the economic, political and military labour that is required to shape them to a useful place in the prevailing order of capitalism:

> If the Southern system of chattel slavery had obstructed industrial progress, provoking a civil war, so the Indian system of communal ownership had inspired resistance to Western expansion; it, too, required destruction and then a policy of 'reconstruction' of the defeated native into the image of their victors: their language and costumes, their names and religion, their laws regarding work and property. (Trachtenberg 1982: 34.)

Equally, functionalist approaches tend to ossify the economic, political and cultural formations of race and class, diverting attention from the trajectory of articulations between race and class: at the economic level, the career of Black America from slavery through debt peonage and 'free' labour to a geographically segregated urban sub-proletariat; and at the political level the sequence of struggles from the destruction of slavery through the fight for non-discriminatory employment to civil rights and the as yet unrealized Rainbow. While it is possible to read race as a gift horse for US capital, providing a powerful axis along which to disorganize class interests among subordinate groups, such an analysis needs to be integrated with an understanding of race as a Trojan Horse: a constantly renewed focal point for organization and struggle.

I want to explore some of these problems of thinking about class formation further by considering the intersection between the growth of industrial capitalism and the place of migrant labour from the late nineteenth century onwards. From an 'economistic' standpoint, the massive influx of migrant labour into the USA was functional for capital in two ways. First, and most obviously, it provided the new labour to fuel the huge expansion of US capitalism at the turn of the century. Secondly, the 'ethnic differentiation' of the migrants provided capital with the free gift of non-economic divisions within the working class, setting in place patterns of suspicion, hostility and antagonism that could cut across the prospect of the forging of working-class unity. As always, such a view treats ethnicity as a free floating or 'epiphenomenal' factor which intrudes from outside onto an essential class formation.

In contrast, social historians have recently returned to study these processes of class and ethnic-cultural formation to argue that a retrospective reading of their 'functional' qualities represses more contradictory relationships (see, for example, Gutman 1977; Trachtenberg 1982; Rosenzweig 1984). Perhaps most significantly, such studies reveal that migrant labour was functional only in the most minimal sense. In addition to their availability for waged labour, migrant workers confronted American capitalism with the problem of how they were to be integrated into the habits of factory labour. This involved the task of 'civilising' migrant groups: in Gramsci's terms, breaking the 'bad habits' of non-industrial life and inculcating the 'good habits' necessary for productive factory labour. Whilst this problem centred most visibly around habits of work (irregularity, poor time keeping, 'Blue Mondays', holidays taken according to the customs of the 'old country', and so on), it by no means stopped there.

Such bad habits were embedded in substantial networks of cultural practices that went far beyond the workplace – into forms of sociability, religion, politics, patterns of domestic economy, sexual divisions of labour, child socialization and linguistic communities. All of these, not just the work habits, became targets for 'reform', the objects of strategies intended to Americanize migrant labour. Such imported cultural practices intersected in complex ways with the drive to forge an American culture. For example, some ethnic cultures brought with them domestic economies which included subsistence production (for example, keeping animals and producing food) which cut across at least three aspects of the American cultural formation. First, in urban and industrial settings, such practices undermined the economic dependence on the wage deemed essential to the cultivation of proper work habits by providing a degree of autonomy from the insistent rhythms of the reproduction of the wage packet. Secondly, such practices interrupted what Braverman called the development of the 'universal market', minimizing dependence on the commodified forms of subsistence, as well as resisting the tendency towards 'cultural universalization' by providing the demands which an ethnic *petit bourgeoisie* could fulfil through the provision of particular foodstuffs, clothing, books, and so on. Thirdly, these domestic economies brought ethnic groups into conflict with emergent state power in such areas as hygiene, domestic orderliness and child rearing (for example, the removal of children from the domestic economy for schooling).

In such ways, then, the cultural formation of migrant labour needs to be seen as a field of contestation where attempts to produce conformity encountered resistances which drew on both the sedimented forms of ethnic culture and the emergent forms available to the migrants in their new setting. Hogan, arguing against a view of 'immigrant cultures' which treats them as static and essential formations, suggests a more dynamic approach:

> In effect, 'immigrant' cultures were creations of the new world not the old; immigrants did not import their ethnicity with them in their suitcases or on their heads. Rather, in confronting the kinds of structural conditions of American society, they created ethnic class cultures ... ethnic cultures are the product of class structuration of social life, a mediation of class cultures. (1982: 41.)

Although underestimating the significance of the sedimented cultural forms which migrants surely did carry with them, Hogan's insistence that ethnic-class cultures are emergent formations is a valuable one. Nevertheless, his formulation might, more properly if less elegantly, identify such formations as ethnic-gender-class cultures, since what was also at stake in

these cultural dynamics was the reorganization of the relations and practices of patriarchal power which were also the
site of civilizing interventions. There are a whole variety of
problems here, which I can sketch only briefly. One aspect
is the destabilization of ethnic forms of patriarchal relations
in the conditions of the new society (and the struggles to
maintain them). Women, as well as men, provided new sources
of waged labour which could undermine ethnic valorizations
of the position of women. The reconstruction of patterns of
domestic economy also involved complex patterns of conflicts
and alliances – for example, in the efforts of white middle-class
women undertaking 'social work', and the attempts of earlier
generations of migrants anxious to teach their newly arrived
cousins the ways of the new world. In leisure, too, ethnic-class
forms of sociability encountered dominant cultural versions of
'respectable pleasures', and the ensuing developments generated new social locations and possibilities for some groups of
women, particularly the young waged, even at the expense of
inter-generational conflicts (Peiss 1986).

Such cultural processes outrun the concepts conventionally
used to analyse them: of which the two dominant ones are
assimilation and cultural pluralism. Assimilation assumes a
static national culture into which ethnic cultures are dissolved.
As such, it makes no allowances for the changes wrought
in the national-popular culture in order to accomplish the
accomodation of ethnic-class cultures. Nor does it have any
space for the way in which such accommodations can sustain
the cultural 'traces' to fuel continuing ethnic-class antagonisms.
In reverse, the concept of cultural pluralism registers only the
co-existence of different cultures, not the degree to which they
interpenetrate in the formation of a national-popular culture,
nor the structures of hierarchy, domination and subordination
which are at stake in the production of the harmony of a
national culture. I think it is more useful to view such a
national-popular culture as a 'unity in difference', in which
alliances, accommodations and even direct repression play roles
in constructing a settlement wherein major contradictions and
antagonisms can be temporarily reconciled or repressed. Such
settlements are necessarily temporary, lasting until the structural
conditions and balance of social forces require their realignment.

The hegemonic creation of 'conformity', the coordination of a whole social formation, has to be continually reworked as the conditions of the society shift. The motors of change are various: the imperatives of capital in economic restructuring; the struggles over political power; and the struggles of subordinate groups against their place in the cultural arena. Such settlements of the national-popular culture are permanently temporary: what Gramsci described as a 'series of unstable equilibria'.

So far I have concentrated attention on the cultural processes associated with migrant labour at the turn of the century, however, I have no wish to imply that such processes were then superseded by a stabilized mass culture and a stable corporate economy. The rise of corporate capital to economic dominance in the early twentieth century, and the complex varieties of coordination which it developed, did not render it secure against new forms of labour organization and militancy in the interwar period, any more than it made it proof against economic crisis or the collapse of finance capital in the Great Depression. Such crises are the most visible examples of the uneven and unstable development of capitalism and also mark the beginnings of the search for new forms of coordination to guard against their recurrence (the search for safer investments, the greater regulation of the financial sector, the range of government intervention under the New Deal, and so on).

Such crises also required renegotiation of the cultural settlement. The complex integration of migrant labour was built around the continuing saga of who was to be included in the American Nation. While groups of migrants were establishing cultures of being Irish-Americans, Polish-Americans, and so forth, their subaltern articulation with America rested on the exclusion of other groups debarred from the melting-pot. The salience of migrant labour and the processes of assimilation have tended to cast the concept of ethnicity in a distinctive way in the USA, such that ethnicity elides the structural differences between European migrants and black Americans. Such differences were symbolically crystallized in the centenary celebrations of the Statue of Liberty in 1986, marking the promise of the 'land of the free' extended to European migrants, but drawing critical comment from black Americans about the different mode of their arrival. The elision of these divergent experiences conceals the extent to which the accommodations made in the integration of European migrant labour rested on the continuing economic, political and cultural exclusion of the black American working class. Through the 1950s and 60s, the accumulated antagonisms of that structure of segregation broke out in both political and cultural forms. The 'Great Society' programmes attempted new accommodations through legal and welfare initiatives, while the national-popular culture was remade to contain elements of black culture, though in limited forms.

Although such developments were political and cultural in form (and, indeed, involved a self-conscious cultural politics), they were also entangled in the economic processes of US capitalism. While taking shape as a politics of ethnicity, the roots lay in the articulation of race and class in postwar affluent America. The economic and political settlement accomplished by Corporate Liberalism in the immediate postwar/Cold War period – the 'truce' between corporate capital and incorporated labour unions – established the basis on which a black ethnic-class culture and politics emerged. The multiple layers of segregation which created a black proletariat and sub-proletariat; which limited their access to and representation by labour unions; which excluded them from political mobilization and representation; and which geographically and culturally isolated the cultures of the ghetto, produced an ethnic politics at this intersection of ethnicity and class formation.

Other elements in the nature of the postwar settlement created the basis for further interruptions in the workings of the land of peace and plenty – this time in the form of feminism. The terms of the postwar settlement were exclusivist in both racial and gender terms. The trajectory of woman's relationship to waged work ran the gamut of contradictory demands: from their rapid wartime entry to 'male' work to their equally rapid postwar expulsion, culminating in discriminatory recruitment back to areas of 'women's work' in the period of postwar expansion. They experienced a simultaneous reconstruction of the other side of women's 'dual role', in the redefinition of domesticity, sexuality and femininity which accompanied the expansion of cultures of consumption. Once again, the accumulated antagonisms, overdetermined by their exclusion from the conventional processes of political representation, established the basis for a cultural politics which privileged gender as its reference point. Here, too, victories were won, compromises made, new grounds for struggle opened up (in particular, around issues of sexuality), and new contradictions of class and ethnicity appeared in the process. In both struggles, one of the outcomes was to deepen class divisions within the groups. The greater recruitment of a black and female middle class since the 1960s went hand in hand with the greater proletarianization and subproletarianization of black people and white women.

STUCK IN THE MIDDLE:
MODES OF COORDINATION

At this point, it is appropriate to return to the problem of the middle classes, because here too there are difficulties attending the attempt to construct static and abstract analyses of class positions which neglect the dynamic and contradictory processes of capitalism. I argued earlier that the task of coordination as a necessary element of a capitalist mode of production was a precondition for thinking about the middle classes. I now want to link this to the preceding arguments about the historical contingency of class formation to suggest a way of approaching the dilemmas which surround the middle classes in Marxist analysis. As a general starting point I offer a brief taxonomy of the elementary forms of the task of coordination in the circuit of capital. These are:

(1) coordination in the person of the individual capitalist (the 'entrepreneurial' mode);
(2) coordination in the form of delegated authority (the 'managerial' mode);
(3) coordination in the form of machinery (the 'technical' mode); and
(4) coordination between competing capitals (the 'professional' mode).

Beginning with the first (and historically prior) form, we may note that there exists an inbuilt tension between the individual control of coordination and the dynamic of capital as a process of expanded reproduction. The expansion of the enterprise poses problems of maintaining direct control over the labour process and of coping with the external conditions of existence (the business environment): the processes of capital creation, distribution, exchange and competition. At this point, we encounter the emergent strategies of capital to cope with expanded reproduction: the incorporation of limited liability companies; concentration (take-overs and mergers); horizontal and vertical integration, and diversification. In their different ways, each involves attempts to secure the conditions of existence: by diversifying and multiplying sources of capital; by minimizing the dangers of competition; by extending control over other aspects of the circuit, and by spreading risks. All such mechanisms displace the possibility of direct coordination. Nevertheless, the entrepreneurial mode continues to play a significant role, not merely as the most powerful ideological metaphor of contemporary capitalism, but as the mode which characterizes much of the self-employed and small business sector (the traditional *petit bourgeoisie*).

The processes of expanded reproduction form the historical preconditions for the development of the 'managerial' mode of coordination: the delegation of tasks of supervision of the labour process to foremen; of the flow of capital to book-keepers and so on. The subsequent splitting and specialization of the managerial function is conditional on the general processes of concentration and diversification, with the growing complexity of both internal and external environments of enterprises and the consequent increased problems of coordination.

The third category of my taxonomy – coordination through machinery – intersects with the second in complex ways. The mechanization (and subsequent automation) of labour processes provides systematic means of controlling the worker (what Marx called the 'real subsumption of labour'). While such control renders the directive role of the labour overseer or foreman increasingly vestigial, it also calls forth new varieties of coordinators: technicians who understand the machines, and managers who understand the integration of the different processes. Each wave of new machinery has produced complex realignments of skill, often with the knowledge being transferred upwards to technical and managerial workers, although later waves have begun to deskill or make redundant lower management levels (for example, the use of information technology in coordinating production processes, stock flows, and so forth).

The fourth category is somewhat different since it is based on the regulation of the relationships between individual capitals, and is intended to guarantee 'fair dealing'. Such guarantees are secured through the intervention of professional formations which are independent of the interests of individual capitals, for example, accounting (in the form of Certified Public Accountants, rather than management accounting) and the law. Such agencies appear to be necessary because competition occasionally gives rise to a propensity to cheat. Through the law in particular, these inter-, rather than intra-, capital modes of coordination intersect with the state: the coordinating agency *par excellence*.[3]

This is, of course, far too brief a comment on both the role of the state and on its place in the expansion of the middle classes. Its coordinative role is extensive: attempting to secure the general conditions of existence for capital accumulation and their reproduction; regulating relations between capitals; coordinating the political relations between classes, and so on. With so much coordinating to be done, the state's substantial contribution to the expansion of the middle classes is not very surprising.[4] I don't suppose that this taxonomy is exhaustive: for example, it leaves out of account a range of pre-capitalist inheritances and their subsequent transformation, such as medicine. Nor do I intend the categories as mutually exclusive (for example, the growth of in-house legal divisions). But I do think that they reveal that coordination provides a useful starting point for thinking about the growth of the middle classes within capitalism. In particular, it provides a point from which to return to Wright's arguments about the middle classes and their location in relations of exploitation.

Although Wright locates the basis of 'organization assets' within the expanded complexity of capitalist labour processes, he nonetheless equates such assets (and their exploitation) with a different mode of production: 'statism'. He also develops a concept of 'skill assets' (and their exploitation) as the basis of a 'socialist' mode of production as a quasi-historical sequence of diminishing bases of class exploitation. Leaving aside the question of whether such a sequencing makes sense, this set of distinctions faces major problems as an account of the middle classes within capitalist societies. It dislocates the middle classes from specifically capitalist social relations, pushing the task of coordination, and its contradictory and dynamic conditions, into the background. There seems little reason to invent a new mode of production to account for a process that is embedded in the logics of an existing one. The case of skill assets is even more confusing. The category of skills (and their equation with credentials) is reified: losing the dynamic place of 'skills' with capitalist societies. Since Braverman's work, it is surely impossible to take skill as a category which has a fixed rather than a historically contingent character. Skills are the product of continuous and coterminous processes of de- and re-skilling. Both organization and skill assets are the effect of capitalist dynamics, which valorize changing forms of knowledge, and which then may be credentialled.

This can be briefly illustrated by reference to the medical profession in the USA. The institutional structures within which medicine is practised have generated the conditions for the establishment of new skills: both in the increasing diversity of medical specialisms (for example, 'emergency medicine') within the hospital labour process, and in the tasks of coordination of that labour process, as in the emergence of medical administration as a credentialled organization asset in the face of the growing concentration and scale of medical practice. More interesting, though, is the impact of the industrialization of medical practice since the 1960s (Wohl 1984), creating diverse conditions for medical work ranging from independent professional through incorporation (group practice) to waged labour employed by major medical companies. While the credentials remain the same, the occupation has acquired a complex set of connections within capitalist social relations as medicine has become increasingly commodified and subject to the constraints of corporate profitability.

Such shifting patterns of skills and credentials (and their labour market consequences) are to be found everywhere in capitalist labour processes, but this dynamic sense of their changing valorization by capital is missing from Wright's analysis. I think that one reason for this tangle of modes of production and reification of assets is to be found in his concern to stabilize Marxist class analysis around the concept of 'exploitation'. Thus, what distinguishes the middle classes is the possession of assets which can be exploited to gain economic advantage over subordinate classes in the distribution of the 'social surplus' in a manner analogous to the advantage belonging to the owners of capital assets. But in spite of a tirade against the failings of Weberian analysis (1984: 106–8), the form of Wright's grappling with the problem of the middle classes concerns precisely those Weberian questions of distribution of advantages in the labour market (the claim on the social surplus manifested in wage/salary differentials). The invention of modes of production based on the exploitation of non-capital assets merely conceals this distributional focus.[5]

The major reason for Wright engaging in this multiplication of exploitations is to be found in his self-criticism of his earlier conceptualization of the middle classes as 'contradictory class locations' (1978). He argues that this approach was flawed by not having the essential Marxist concept of exploitation at its centre, stressing instead the issues of power and domination being exercised over subordinate classes. Power does not meet the requirements of being an essential Marxist concept for the analysis of modes of production and the elementary structure of classes. (A similar argument against power is deployed by Wolff and Resnick, 1986.) This flight from the concept of power has real intellectual and political imperatives. It is possible to sympathize with the Marxists' reluctance to use the concept in the post-Foucault world, where power has come to play the role of the Scarlet Pimpernel: here, there, everywhere – and eternally elusive. Such sympathy is, however, reduced by the suspicion that the refusal of power is intended to help insulate the purity of class analysis from the threat of contamination by analyses of race and gender which have given a central role to the concept of power.

The difficulty seems to me to arise from the excessive weight that is being given to the concept of mode of production. While it is true that at this level the concept of power is not needed to specify the social relations of production: the mode of production does not contain all the concepts necessary for class analysis. Power remains an element of class analysis in that it identifies capacities exercised and struggled over by classes. The task of coordination can be specified at the level of the mode of production, but its execution requires the exercise of power over those whose work is to be coordinated. There is a difficult problem to be faced in thinking through the different modes of power, sites of use and sets of relations in which it is effective: but that is not to say that it cannot be used in a 'properly' Marxist analysis. Each mode of power – managerial, politico-juridical or patriarchal – has its own field of operation and its own distinctive relationships. At the same time, however, there are connections between them: both managerial and patriarchal power have definite links with the legal authority of the State.[66]

I do not for a moment suppose that these observations have settled the problem of the middle classes, but I believe that by insisting on the dynamics of class formation and the place of coordination within those dynamics, the problem might reappear in a more manageable – and useful – form.

MIDDLE AMERICA:
IMAGES OF THE GOOD LIFE

Although conceptual and definitional differences abound, most commentators seem to agree that the last 30 years have seen a substantial expansion of the American middle classes, both in public and private sector employment. That expansion has included some shifts in the racial and gender distribution of middle-class employment, predominantly, though not exclusively, through the expansion of state employment in the 1960s and 70s. Both public and private sector expansions have been the object of extensive analysis and new conceptual initiatives. The expansion of the state sector has given rise to the exploration of the concept of the 'new class', primarily by neo-conservative analysts, while terms such as the 'service class' have been deployed in discussions of the expansion of the commercial middle class in order to capture the process as being one not just of expansion but of changing composition.[7] The qualitative nature of these changes lies in the growing salience of the sphere of circulation: retailing, marketing and advertising as one nexus and financial services as another.

These changes mark a distinctive shift in the problems of coordination which confront US capital (and are reflected in other advanced capitalist economies) from a focus on the coordination of production to that of markets (both those of capital formation and of retail). Such changes parallel the recomposition of domestic capital and, in particular, the tendency towards the exporting of production to low wage economies outside the USA itself. Whether such fractions constitute a service class in any meaningful sense seems debatable. They do, of course, perform services for capital, but are by no means unique in that. What does distinguish them from other fractions of the middle classes is that the forms of coordination which they provide centre around the work of symbolic manipulation – both in the cultural sphere and in the financial markets. Reich (1984) has drawn attention to these tendencies' growing domination of the world of American management: most visibly in the form of what he has called 'paper entrepreneurialism'. Nonetheless, the tasks of coordinating both consumer and financial markets remain forms of delegated managerial control, even though the specific forms of expertise, and their relative dominance, may be distinctive. Viewed from this standpoint, the issue of whether such forms of delegated coordination take place in house or are bought in as external sources of expertise does not affect the nature of the function *vis-a-vis* capital. It may, though, have consequences for the cultural formation of such expertise. For example, external concentrations of expertise (such as advertising and marketing agencies) may underline self-conceptions of creative autonomy and service provision.

Both the increased salience of the sphere of circulation and the particular forms of expertise centering around symbolic manipulation of various kinds do mark a shift in the formation of the middle classes, and this shift is reflected in new forms of middle-class culture, condensed in the 1980s imagery of 'yuppies'(young upwardly mobile professionals). In brief, these new middle-class fractions have been the focal point for a heightened involvement in consumption, the promotion of cultural cosmopolitanism, and the centrality of lifestyle as the nexus of cultural consumption. This formation has been the hegemonic element in American national-popular culture during the 1980s – both continuing and reforming the place of middle–class culture within the national-popular.

American national-popular culture has historically been dominated by the cultural forms and imagery of the middle class, although its specific cultural formations have changed extensively. For example, the twentieth century has seen movements from a populist competitive individualism to the corporate liberalism of the 1950s through to the current cosmopolitan consumer culture. Each of these has played the hegemonic role in the formation of the national-popular culture in different periods. Each has posed itself as a distinctive version of the American dream. There are other continuities, too. In each, the home has been a central locus for the articulation of the 'good life', although shifting in its connotations from respectability to suburban bliss to display case. Equally importantly, each has articulated a version of American liberalism: from the competitive individualism of the 'little man' (sic) to the corporate liberalism of the 'organization man' (sic) to the economic and cultural libertarianism of the lifestyle 1980s.[8]

These varieties of liberalism index major shifts in the composition of the middle classes, though their hegemonic self-confidence provides a cohering thread. The economic remaking of the middle classes through the rising significance of the sphere of circulation took place alongside a social remaking of their race and gender composition. The emergence of a black middle class (albeit rather small) and the professional woman have had their effects on the cultural repertoire of the new middle classes, breaking its historical alignment with domesticated white suburbia, and posing new problems of accommodation of hitherto subordinated groups within the national-popular culture.

Even allowing for such changes, the contemporary formation of middle-class culture remains dominated by the association with forms of symbolic manipulation. The new middle classes have constructed a system of equivalences between their economic functions and their cultural formation. Symbolic manipulation underpins these equivalences, along with the focus on creativity (as the production of difference), and the promotion of lifestyle as the purpose of consumption.

Cosmopolitanism thus indexes the self-conception of worldly sophistication and the imperial sense of the world as a field of cultural resource through which the project of the self can be constructed. This cosmopolitanism distinguishes the new fractions most clearly from the cultural formations of their predecessors which were organized around more self-consciously American elements. This cultural libertarianism, associated with an economic libertarianism, provides both points of articulation with contemporary American political culture, and the points of difference from traditional cultural formations which have greeted the new cosmopolitanism in tones of offence and outrage.

It is only this constructed equivalence of economic function and cultural formation which gives me pause for thought about the concept of the 'service class'. What better service could be sought from a class fraction than that it should be simultaneously the exemplary consumer (with a profound psychic and economic investment in consumption as the means of producing the self) and occupy the commanding heights of the means of constructing and transmitting the messages about the meaning of consumption? In such terms, the new middle classes look like the ideal subaltern class, living out their sense of mission in work and play. Such dedicated service deserves – and has thus far earned – its rewards. Davis has pointed to the political promotion of a culture of 'overconsumption' through the subsidization of the 'sub-bourgeois' (1986: 211), arguing that through the 1970s and early 80s: 'political trends have tended to unify corporate capital and most of the new middle strata in a strategy of cost-displacement towards the working and unwaged poor.' (1986: 219.)

Such an alliance was a necessary precondition for the recomposition of US capital during the 1970s and 80s to escape from the declining profitability of the Fordist ensemble of domestic manufacture for mass domestic markets. The escape rested on both the liberation of capital itself and the improved coordination of the sphere of circulation in both financial and consumer markets: the focal points of the new middle-class fractions. In that alliance are condensed the economic, political and cultural problems which these fractions pose for any analysis of the present conjuncture.

AN INCONCLUSIVE CONCLUSION

The following two chapters are concerned with cultures of consumption and the political formation of the American New Right respectively, and these issues will be pursued therein. For the moment, I wish to concentrate on drawing together the threads of the argument of this chapter concerning class and its cultural formation. It has been my intention to challenge essentialist views of class formation by drawing out the dynamic and contingent conditions in which class is linked to other social relations, particularly those of race and gender. Such a position does not mean surrendering the effectivity of class relations – the social dynamics of a capitalist mode of production – but it does mean that considerations of social and cultural formations cannot presume that class is either their only, or even their dominant, focal point. In reverse, neither racial nor gender relations persist untouched by the effects of capitalist dynamics: all three coexist, bound together in an uneasy and contradictory ensemble. While each element may have its own distinctive trajectory, such that patriarchal or racial forms of power and differentiation are not reducible to those of capitalism, each necessarily works through the others. However avidly it may be sought by the purist, the unraced and ungendered class will not be discovered.

I also wish to briefly draw attention to the implications of such a contingent view of class formation for the concept of culture, in part because it is in the non-economic realms that race and gender have been most fully delineated as axes of social differentiation. Such cultural formations of class-race-gender identities and practices are not to be neglected by Marxists because of their 'superstructural' character, nor be subjected to distinctions between class consciousness and non-class identities. The formation of a national-popular culture may, or may not, be articulated around class identities, but still needs to be considered as the field within which class and other antagonisms are played out. This last point bears as much on the place of the middle classes within Marxist analysis as it does on the traditional subject, the proletariat. I have tried to sketch an account of the economic and cultural significance of the middle classes, based on a concept of the capitalist mode of production as problematic and processual, as well as relational, which highlights the problems of coordination. By doing so, I hope to have combined an insistence on the continuing value of central Marxist concepts with an attention to the historical dynamics of the processes of cultural formation. That combination seems to me to be a necessary one. If we keep in mind that capitalism, even in its abstract theorization, is an unstable and contradictory process, it may help to avoid forcing the concrete analysis of historical conjunctures into ill-fitting straitjackets of conceptual rigour.

NOTES

This chapter was originally drafted in Madison, Wisconsin, in April 1986, and has been improved considerably through the assistance of comments from and discussions with Leslie Roman, Allen Hunter, Les Meyer, Janet Newman, Cameron McCarthy and Paul du Gay.

1 The distinction between organic and conjunctural is taken from Gramsci, and reflects his concern with being able to identify points of political effectivity. Wright's disregard for diachronic analysis may derive from the tension of combining Marxist theory with the techniques and concerns of empirical sociology.

2 The emergence of new social histories concerned with local class, ethic and gender formations has been important in opening up such issues, and undercuts many of the assumptions of functionalist analyses of class relations. See, for example, Rosenzweig (1984); Gutman (1977); Peiss (1986) and also McDowell and Massey (1984), on geographical variations of class and gender formations.

3 The imagery of the professional mode, especially its independence, has been a powerful influence on the formation of both state and private sector service providers (Johnson 1972).

4 This rather flippant treatment of the state is not intended to underestimate its importance, either politically or in relation to the formation of the middle classes. Nonetheless, the topic of the form and consequences of the state in Marxist analysis is too extensive to be pursued here.

5 This is a structural feature of the approach to exploitation which Wright adopts from Roemer (1982) which adopts a zero-sum game theoretic model for examining exploitation, and derives from a neo-classical view of rationally calculating economic individuals. As such it bears little resemblance to the process of exploitation based on the pre-, rather than post-, production

distribution of the means of production. See Marx on the different distributions, (1973: 94–6).

6   One of the more irritating features of Foucault's critique of Marxism's focus on state power is his willingness to forget just how extensively the various discourses of subjection are both dependent on, and contribute to the extension of, state power. This is concealed by his narrow equation of Marxist concepts of the state with the 'repressive' juridical structures.

7   Both concepts have European antecedents. The neo-conservative identification of a 'new class' among state professionals and bureaucrats is derived from Djilas' work (1957) on bureaucracies in state socialist societies; while the origin of the concept of the 'service class' is to be found in the work of Karl Renner (1978).

8   The varieties of middle-class culture (and the varieties of liberalism articulated within it) might be traced through such authors as Trachtenberg (1982) and Jackson Lears (1983) for the late nineteenth and early twentieth centuries; Reisman (1961), Wright Mills (1956) and Biskind (1983) for the postwar decades. For contemporary variants, see, *inter alia*, Maddox and Lillie (1984) on libertarianism; Hunter (1988); and Grossberg (1988).

4

'Mine eyes dazzle': cultures of consumption

One of the most striking features of the development of American society has been the creation of 'mass consumption'. Although patterns of mass consumption have been reproduced in other Western metropolitan societies, the USA appears as both the most developed and the leading case – not least because of the processes of economic and cultural diffusion which have linked the European societies to the consumer culture of the USA. The development of mass consumption has become a central issue in the analysis of American culture because of the way in which subordinate social groups have been inserted in to the promises of mass consumption and into the social identity of consumers. For the most part, critical analyses of this system of consumption have portrayed it as having a deadening and depoliticizing weight on the possibilities of a radical culture of opposition within the USA, and as having destroyed the collective bases of class and community identity necessary to sustain such opposition. In place of those collective identities, mass consumption has created a culture of atomized, depoliticized individuals who can seek satisfaction and identity only through the market place. More recently, there has emerged an alternative strain of cultural analysis which has represented consumption as an active and creative social practice, and as the site of resistances among subordinated social groups. This chapter explores the tensions between these two views in considering how cultures of consumption can be a site both for the construction of hegemony and for popular resistances.

BUYING IN:
AMERICANIZATION AS CONSUMPTION

The recent development of critical cultural history in the USA has created a substantial reassessment of the relationship between class and ethnicity in the late nineteenth and early twentieth century formation of the American working class. These studies have highlighted the way in which the complex ethnic composition of the working class, fuelled by waves of migrant labour, has acted not merely as a source of division and fragmentation but also as a resource for collective action and class solidarity. Whilst the repertoires of ethnic cultures were doubtless remade during the process of turning migrant workers into wage labourers, they continued to provide sources of identity and resilience in the face of the new habits of body and mind demanded by their employers. In some cases, these collective resistances took place around the issues of work, resulting in refusals to succumb to new patterns of time and work discipline, or to the prerogatives of owners and managers in the control of the labour process. Such struggles were both informal and formal, from the 'bloodymindedness' of workers who maintained 'Saint Monday' as a rest day, to the creation of labour unions (Gutman 1977). In other cases, the same mix of class relations and ethnic cultures manifested itself in struggles over access to and control of free time away from the workplace, affecting public and private practices of leisure (Rosenzweig 1984).

One recurrent theme of such studies, however, is the transition from localized class-ethnic cultural formations to a new phase in the development of American society: the arrival of a national mass culture embodied in the creation of mass media of entertainment (film and radio) and in the growth of systems of mass production, distribution and consumption (for example, in clothing and food). These changes undermined the collective practices and identities of class-ethnic cultures and created the overarching social identity of the American consumer.

Rosenzweig's study (1984) of the struggles over leisure in Worcester, Massachusetts, identifies the shift from the nickelodeon to the movie palace as one of the turning-points in this transition. This change condensed three processes: first,the change in the production and content of films associated with the growth of the studio system; second, the greater economic integration of production and distribution; and third, the changes created in the social practices of film viewing in the attempt to make film-going a 'respectable' (that is, non-proletarian) leisure pursuit. Rosenzweig highlights the 'cultural work' which went into broadening the class basis of the film watching public to include the middle-classes in terms of the changing content of films, the new architecture of the cinema, and the assertion of decorum over the social behaviour of the cinema audiences themselves, involving the suppression of forms of collective sociability which had characterized working-class participation in the nickelodeon.

Stuart and Elizabeth Ewen's *The Channels of Desire* (1982) also identifies reconstruction of the cinema as one of the turning points in the development of a culture of consumption that took an audience of young immigrant workers (particularly young women) away from films whose content was responsive to their experience of America, into the Hollywood structures of desire and identity. The new cinema offered a guide to the American Dream: a dream which could be realized through consumption. Parallel to development of the cinema, the Ewens trace the rise of systems of mass production and distribution (especially of clothing) which provided the commodities through which the dream might be fulfilled. The Ewens argue that these processes dissolved the cultural patterns of class differentiation into the mass symbolism of the market-place. In doing so, they dislocated collective and communal identities, erecting in their place wholly individualized relationships between consumers, their dreams and the market's realm of commodities:

> Mass imagery . . . creates for us a memorable language, a system of belief, an ongoing channel to inculcate and effect common perceptions, explaining to us what it means to be part of the 'modern world'. It is a world defined by the retail (individualized) consumption of goods and services; a world

in which social relations are often disciplined by the exchange of money; a world where it increasingly **makes sense** that if there are solutions to be had, they can bought. (1982: 42; emphasis in original.)

Fox and Lears (eds 1983) also treat the emergence of mass consumption as marking a decisive shift in the nature of American culture. Although their analysis attempts to reserve a greater place for an active model of the consumer, their main argument concerns the reorganization of a Protestant culture in order to dismantle the psychological inhibitions against consumption, conspicuous display and self-expression. They suggest that the culture of consumption had its foundation in the development of corporate capitalism from entrepreneurial capitalism, leading to the rise of a professional and managerial service class. It was this class, they argue, which led the reconstruction of American middle-class culture towards a new culture which stressed 'therapeutic consumption' and permitted 'pervasive self absorption' (1983: xii).

While these studies differ in their precise angle of approach to the study of mass consumption, they share some common features. Firstly, they identify links between the political and cultural effects of mass consumption and its basis in the rise of systems of mass production in the USA in the early twentieth century, particularly those systems geared to servicing a newly created domestic market. Secondly, they see this culture of consumption as a national (and nationalizing) phenomenon which displaced earlier forms of cultural, social and political practice (although they differ as to what was displaced). Thirdly, they see the creation of the consumer as the making of a new dominant identity in American society which displaces or at least demotes other forms of identification. This process of displacement towards the consumer identity has politically demobilizing effects and contributes to the making of a new form of capitalist hegemony in the USA that links the economy, culture and the psychic structures of the individual. Before I consider some of the implications of these analyses, and contrast them with alternative approaches, I wish to draw attention to one particular peculiarity about their treatment of consumption.

A MATTER OF MOMENTS:
CONSUMPTION, EXCHANGE AND THE COMMODITY

For all their concern with the culture of consumption, it is, in fact, very difficult to find any analysis of consumption itself in these studies. Consumption as a social practice remains largely invisible. What the analyses focus upon is the apparatus, mechanisms and cultural significance of the market-place. By this I mean that these studies are less concerned with how people consume the commodities they have purchased, than with the fact that the commodities are purchased. This gives too narrow a meaning to consumption. The general Marxist analysis of the capitalist mode of production sees the 'circuit of capital' as made up of a number of different moments: production, distribution, exchange and consumption. What these analyses of consumption actually address is the moment of *exchange*: the process of purchasing commodities (or commodified services) in the market. They deal very little with what the consumer does with those commodities after they have been purchased and removed (for private use) from the market-place. The process they describe – the growth of mass consumption – is the one which Harry Braverman (1974) described as the spread of the 'universal market': the incorporation of more and more areas of social activity into market relations, so that increasingly people come to purchase the means of consumption.

In identifying the development of mass consumption as a major shift in the structure and culture of American society, these views of consumption collapse together two different analytical moments (exchange and consumption) and treat them as if they were identical. The effect of this is to read off the practice of consumption from the generalized conditions of exchange relationships. In reality, consumption takes place after – and separate from – the act of exchange (or its illegitimate substitutes, such as theft). The result is to equate the cultural and political qualities of the act of exchange with the act of consumption as if they were inseparable. The implication of this is that the cultural meaning of consumption is always pre-given, determined by its location within exchange relations, and inscribed in the character of the commodities being purchased.

These critiques of consumer culture draw (implicitly or explicitly) on Marx's analysis of 'commodity fetishism' in Chapter 1 of *Capital*, in which he argues that the production and exchange of commodities in capitalism means that the 'social relation between men ... assumes ... the fantastic form of a relation between things' (1976: 165). This process of mystification obscures the social relations of production though which commodities are created, such that real human labour becomes objectified in a fantastic world of objects. Social relationships become mediated by this realm of objects, and in particular by the 'master commodity' – money – through which the processes of exchange are conducted. This analysis of commodity fetishism is implicit in the argument about the ways in which consumer culture displaces issues of need and identity into the individualized realm of consumption. 'Satisfaction' can only be achieved through the purchase of commodities, in which the self can be realized (albeit in distorted and fetishised forms).[1]

The political implications of this view of commodity fetishism are fairly obvious. It points to the inextricable link between the 'enrichment' of the magical world of commodities and the simultaneous impoverishment of human social relationships. The spread of the 'universal market' from the early twentieth century has meant that fields of social activity that were previously domestic or communal practices have been subsumed into the cash-nexus of exchange relations (food, sport, entertainment, clothing), alongside the generation of 'new needs' which can only be serviced through the market (of which 'cultural commodities' such as films, records, and television, might be the best examples). In this process, human relations are mystified and wrenched apart by the intervention of the commodities which capitalism produces. The same mode of production which creates 'alienated labour' in the process of production, also generates alienation in the sphere where capitalism promises that the self can be realized: the realm of 'private freedom' in consumption. The promises of satisfaction and self-realization paraded in the dazzling display of the market-place constantly offer the chance to overcome the alienated condition: you can become whatever you wish to be. Thus the culture of consumption – in terms of its psychological economy – is a permanent force for expansion. The next promise must be sought to overcome the sense of dissatisfaction resulting from the previous one. The destruction of earlier forms of communal and collective identity ensures that only the market-place can offer this prospect of transcending dissatisfaction, even though it is always doomed to perpetual failure and the re-creation of frustration.

Such analyses of mass consumption often assume a homology between the economic and cultural powers of capital. The commodity is seen to have a stabilized or fixed single meaning, which is inscribed in the commodity during its production. This meaning is transferred to the consumer through the exchange process. This 'transfer of meaning' completes the hegemonic circuit associated with mass consumption, since in purchasing the commodity, the consumer also 'buys into' the dominant ideology of American capitalism. Thus, for example, the Ewens' tracing of the rise of Hollywood and its effect on film content sets out the processes by which a film culture, open to diverse cultural meanings and responsive to the cultures of subordinate groups, displaces those concerns in favour of the creation of a dominant set of representations of America. There are problems associated with this conception of the stability of meaning in commodities, and it is precisely the instability of meaning that provides the basis for cultural analyses which stress consumption as an active and creative cultural process. This problem will be more fully explored in what follows, but some of its implications can be identified in the changing evaluations of the Hollywood melodrama. The genre has been critically denigrated as a 'weak' popular form, associated with oppressive narratives of romance and pejoratively viewed as 'women's films'. More recently, feminist analyses have reclaimed melodrama, arguing that it is one of the few film genres to feature strong and autonomous women characters and engaging concerns which are repressed or marginalized in more 'masculine' genres. Such alternative readings demonstrate the problems of assuming that there is one single and stabilized meaning associated with a commodity or text. However, to argue that there is not one single meaning is to open up a whole new set of problems.

SIGN WARS:
SYMBOLS OF RESISTANCE

The cultural and political pessimism of such views of mass consumption contrasts with a different tradition within cultural studies which sees the social practice of consumption as the site of resistance to incorporation into dominant meanings. Studies in this vein have treated culture as a field of class (and other) conflict, and have stressed the active role which subordinate groups play in creating cultures and subcultures of resistance and refusal. One major strand of this approach has been the emergence of a cultural history following E. P. Thompson's *The Making of the English Working Class* (1963). Thomson's work opened the door for studies of the working class which went beyond the traditional work-place based concerns of labour history. This new cultural history has explored the complex relations between dominant and subordinate groups engaged in cultural struggle, examining in particular the interplay between class, ethnicity and gender in the shaping of the turn-of-the-century working class. Such studies have insisted on the recurrent capacity of subordinate groups to 'make themselves' as well as be made by the processes of US capitalism. They have stressed the diverse sources and forms of opposition, ranging from collective organization to the informal subcultures of 'disorderliness' which attracted constant efforts to discipline, regulate and reconstruct in order 'civilize' the lower orders. (See Butsch, ed., 1990, for an overview.)

Subordinate cultures were the site of the maintenance, revitalization and reconstruction of communal identities through cultural practice. Based around such focal points as bars, social clubs, sports, holidays, and the uses of public space, they involved forms of consumption which resisted direct incorporation into the patterns of the dominant culture. For example, Rosenzweig (1984) has traced the ways in which a mixture of informal collective organization and the use of local commercial facilities (especially drinking places) created a culture of leisure which embodied subordinate class and ethnic interests and concerns in nineteenth century Worcester. Kathy Peiss (1986) has examined the role played by the 'cheap amusements' of early commercial leisure provision in providing spaces in which young working women could develop autonomous forms of cultural practice taking them outside the traditional confines of family authority. Both Rosenzweig and Peiss are conscious of the ways in which these cultures of resistance are less than counter-hegemonic – that they are resistances within the wider structures of American capitalism and patriarchy. They nevertheless demonstrate forms of cultural practice in which members of subordinate groups live their subordination in active and contradictory ways. This subordination is not the outcome of a one dimensional – and one directional – incorporation; but is based on a contradictory dynamic of incorporation and resistance.

It may be argued that since the end result of these processes is the reproduction of subordination, the precise nature of such cultural practices is largely irrelevant. However, I want to insist that it makes both a political and a theoretical difference as to whether we see subordinate groups as monolithically integrated into a dominant culture; or as enmeshed in a field of active cultural resistance, negotiation and compromise, requiring continuing 'ideological work' to maintain that subordination. It is this conception of hegemony, as a continuing and contradictory process, that is the core of Gramsci's view of the relationship between ideology and 'common sense', in opposition to a view of hegemony as the unilateral imposition of a unified dominant culture.

It might also be argued that these studies are primarily of historical interest, in that they deal with 'pre-corporate' structures of production and consumption, before the deluge of mass consumption. They can be seen as merely detailing those forms of collective and communal practice which were first subverted and then supplanted by the the processes of massification and individualization that accompanied the culture of consumption. While this is true in terms of periodization, it is a far less satisfactory argument in terms of the dynamic view of domination and resistance which are the heart of such studies. Analyses of mass consumption have tended to focus on the systems of representation built into consumption: the dominant meanings embodied in the imagery of advertising, the rhetoric of corporate production, and the significance attached to particular commodities. As Fox and Lears put it:

Most recent social history has focused on the cultures of
the common people, a previously neglected subject. But it is
impossible to understand the cultures of ordinary Americans
without appreciating the ways those cultures are influenced
and delimited by the ideals, plans and needs of the powerful.
(1983: x.)

At one level, this argument is powerfully persuasive. The 'cultures of the common people' do not take shape in a vacuum,
separated from the structures of economic, political and cultural
power. But there is a reverse danger which needs to be taken
into account. In studying the 'ideals, plans, and needs of the
powerful' we can too readily assume that ordinary Americans
play the roles they are allocated in those plans, and that the
plans work as intended. To treat intentions as outcomes in this
way is to lapse into a highly fatalistic form of functionalism,
involving a conception of the power of the powerful which has
no space for refusal, resistance or even negotiation.

The emergence of cultural studies in Britain and North America has been marked by a commitment to studying the 'cultures
of the common people' (or popular culture) in contemporary
as well as historical settings. Much of this work testifies to the
gap between the plans and needs of the powerful and the lived
practices of subordinate groups. Many of these studies have
focused on the 'subcultural worlds' of the young (originally
of young working-class males, but subsequently extended to
adolescent girls and middle-class youth, see Hall and Jefferson,
eds., 1976, Muncie 1985 and McRobbie and Nava, eds 1984).
These subcultural studies have insisted that culture, and the
creation of collective social identities within it, need to be
viewed as an active social process. Youth subcultures, for
example, involve a set of signifying practices concerning language, music, clothes, social space and sexuality. This body
of work has produced a major reassessment of youth culture,
challenging the conception of it as a generational phenomenon
based in biological and psychological processes of maturation,
and offering an alternative view which sees it as a fractured
world of subcultural practices in which the social relations of
class, race and gender are both reproduced and played with
in forms of symbolic creativity. These studies have constantly

emphasized the plasticity of commodities: their capacity for being subverted, challenged, and reworked to mean something new (of which punk's spectacular uses of mundane objects may be the most dramatic example). (See Hebdige 1979 and Chambers 1986.)

Such arguments have considerable significance for the study of cultures of consumption, even though they are open to a variety of criticisms.[2] Firstly, they provide a continuing testimony that if hegemony is accomplished, it is not a pre-given and stable process. The implications of such studies are Gramscian in their insistence on treating hegemony as a constant and contradictory process in which subordinate groups are necessarily active participants, not passive victims. Secondly, they provide a view of consciousness as partial, uneven and contradictory. Although the subcultural identities constructed by working-class males may be developed through a cultural repertoire that defines class against race (a **white** working class) and through gender (a **male** working class), this does not undermine the significance of the construction of class identities. It does, of course, raise problems about their definition of class, and about the political tasks of overcoming such fragmentation, but that is still a different starting point from one in which class did not even appear in the cultural repertoire. Thirdly, and most significantly in this context, such studies insist that consumption is not a passive process, but an active one involving the cultural work of signifying practice which puts to use the polysemic quality of the commodity-as-sign: the capacity of a sign to be made to mean different things. The use of the commodity is not absolutely inscribed into it at the point of production, and the possibility of alternative uses cannot be completely closed off. The significance of a white tee shirt changes depending on whether it is worn for insulation under a Brooks Brother shirt, or (post James Dean) above a pair of blue denims, even though the economic profit may be exactly the same.

More recently, the implications of this subcultural analysis have been developed into a more thorough-going view of consumption in the era of consumer culture as a self-conscious critique of the pessimistic view of mass consumption (see, for example, Myers 1986). The stress on creativity and polysemy has been allied to concepts derived from textual analysis, especially those of pleasure and the ways in which texts offer different subject positions. The fruits of this combination are approaches to consumption which stress the active role of the consumer in creating the meaning of the object or text being consumed. Individuals are cast as cultural *bricoleurs*, assembling their own distinctive combinations of style from the treasury of available signifiers. At the heart of this view of consumption is the process of differentiation – both theoretically, in terms of meaning being generated through signification as the construction of differences, and practically, in the social process of consumption being seen as the production and display of difference in life style, taste and politics. Everyone, in this argument, is a cultural expert: using and manipulating the symbols of everyday culture.

> In this collage of sights and sounds [of the contemporary scene] we discover the immediate coordinates of the present: where existing meanings and views, ideas and opinions are reproduced; where social practices are formed and experienced; where both consensus and rebellion are voiced; where dogma and innovation, prejudice and change find expression.
>
> Contemporary urban culture, then, is a complex cypher of its circumstances. Across its multiple surfaces a popular semiotics mixes together real conditions and imaginary material. The vivid languages of the cinema, television, pop music and magazines are translated into personalized styles, manners, tastes and pleasures: under given conditions, in particular situations, we take reality to pieces in order to put it back together with a further gain in meaning. The signs are inhabited, appropriated, domesticated. (Chambers, 1986: 185.)

These explorations of consumption as cultural creativity involve theoretical gains over the pessimistic views of mass consumption discussed earlier. They establish that consumption as a social practice cannot be read off directly from the processes of exchange and that consciousness is not determined directly by the commodities that are consumed. They insist on the necessity of seeing social subjects as active agents in their own creation, rather than the passive victims of capitalism. And yet, there are aspects of this view of consumption which leave me uneasy, although in a very different way from the earlier pessimism. Some of this uneasiness relates to the way this view of consumption inverts the errors of the pessimists. Where the mass consumption analyses tend to focus on the moment of exchange and ignore the practice of consumption, this view of cultural creativity highlights consumption as an active social practice and relegates exchange and commodity relations to the background. What we see is the excess of signs, not the conditions of production, distribution and exchange which make them available. The effect, ironically, is to replicate that view of capitalism which capitalism would most like us to see: the richness of the market-place and the freely choosing consumer. The other side – the structures of production and the inequalities of access to the market-place – are missing, and these absences emphasize the 'free-floating' quality of the sign, making it available for any use or meaning that may be attached to it.

At a less abstract level, there are other sources of unease. I cannot help feeling that there is something headily romantic about this view of consumption which leaves out of account the less glamourous experience of consuming in the contemporary world. It is focused on consumption as *bricolage*: the assemblage of meanings, statements and lifestyles. What there does not seem to be space for is the more mundane experiences of subsistence consumption. These cultural *bricoleurs* do not feel as though they are pushing prams around while trying to keep to the week's budget. This does not mean that subsistence consumption has been unaffected by the changes in the culture of consumption: the geographical, cultural and economic restructurings of the retail sector have effects on all consumers. But whether all consumers have the same access to these possibilities of creativity or all experience the same pleasures of consuming is another matter.

Last, but not necessarily least, there is an uncomfortable way in which this view of consumption is attuned to the spirit of the age. It both reflects and adds emphasis to the shift towards consuming individualism and away from the realm of collective. public and political agency. I do not mean that its view of consumption is uncritical, but that it accepts the shift of cultural and political terrain towards consumption as the new ground for analysis rather than keeping open the tensions between consumption and other sites and other modes of power, control and creativity. Judith Williamson has highlighted the diminished realm of power and control associated with consumption:

> The conscious, chosen meaning in most people's lives comes much more from what they consume than what they produce. Clothes, interiors, furniture, records, knick-knacks, all the things we buy involve decisions and the exercise of our own judgement, choice, 'taste'. Obviously, we don't choose what is available for us to choose between in the first place. Consuming seems to offer a certain scope for creativity, rather like a toy where all the parts are pre-chosen but the combinations are multiple.
>
> Ownership is at present the only form of control legitimized in our culture. (Williamson 1983: 230–31.)

What concerns me about the current attention being given to consumption is its reinforcement of this legitimation – as though consumption was the only site or form of control to which attention should be given rather than exploring its intersection with other sites where struggles for control have been marginalized or de-legitimized.

For me, neither the exchange/commodity based view of consumerism nor the view of consumption-as-social practice is, by itself, a satisfactory way of analysing consumption. The structural pessimism of the former finds it mirror image in the cultural optimism of the latter, leaving us to choose between a view of people as broken spirits or free spirits. Since neither seems a satisfactory view of the contradictory ways people have to find for 'living with capitalism', I want to explore these tensions through the interconnection of production, exchange and consumption in the making of contemporary 'cultures of consumption' of Western capitalism.[3]

AFFORDING IT: THE POLITICAL ECONOMY OF MASS CONSUMPTION

The emergence of mass consumption marked a distinctive shift in the social and economic organization of Western capitalism.

They represented a profound restructuring of the processes of production, distribution, exchange and consumption, and in the ways in which these processes intersected. Changes in patterns and practices of consumption rested on (and contributed to) the restructuring of production itself through the innovations of Taylorism and Fordism as managerial strategies designed to improve the productivity and controllability of labour, including what Marx called the 'real subsumption of labour': the subjection of labour to the discipline of the machine. The enhanced productivity set free by these innovations from the turn of the century onwards necessitated the expansion of existing markets and the discovery of new ones: central among which was to be the domestic market of the working class.

Davis (1986) calls this set of developments 'Fordism', highlighting the integral links between the emergence of mass consumption and the development of mass production and the high wage economy instituted by Ford in his 'five dollar day'. Fordism as a concept in Marxist analysis has generally been directed towards a focus on the systems of production, but the high wage economy is a crucial link between the reorganization of production on the one hand and the enabling of the working class to develop new patterns of consumption on the other. The increase of domestic mass consumption is both an effect of the reorganization of capitalist production, and a precondition for its greater expansion.

It is misleading to focus on the reorganization of processes of production in a narrow sense alone, since the expansion of consumption has also involved the reorganization of the processes of distribution and exchange. These changes have had particular significance given the geographical structure of the United States. Without the distributive infrastructure provided by the railway system and the creation of an integrated postal system (essential for mail order distribution), domestic consumption would necessarily have remained dependent on localized sets of production and exchange. Both the mail order systems and the new urban 'palaces of consumption' – the department stores – demonstrate striking parallels between the rationalization of work processes in production and distribution. Alan Trachtenberg has pointed out the principles which governed the internal order of the department store:

The form itself of the early stores betrayed the calculation within the spectacle: a complex machinery of accounting and coordination, of stockkeeping and purchase order, of hierarchy and control, that lay behind the glittering facade, the ceremonial entrances, the bright interiors, all suggesting a kind of magical appearance of goods as if from nowhere . . . And the relation to the factory was omnipresent, organic and reciprocal. Behind the monumental fronts and beneath the surface elegance lay a design almost strictly analogous to that emerging in the larger factories under the influence of electricity, a design of specialized spaces and functions . . . Like the factory, the multiple-product store came in the 1880s to count less on economies of scale and more on velocity, on efficiency of movement from distribution point to warehouse to store: from stock to counter to sale . . . Department stores, because of economic necessity, installed the principles of productivity at the very heart of the city. (1982: 133–4.)

This intersection between the public 'magic' of display and a tightly integrated labour process also involved a newly recruited, and predominantly female, labour force. These developments also began to affect the nature of exchange relationships; the practice of being a consumer. As almost everyone writing about department stores has observed, the new stores (and in their own ways the movie palace and the mail order catalogue) locate the moment of buying in the realm of spectacle: both the commodities themselves and their 'settings' are made spectacular. What is more striking is the intersection between this ' fabulous realm' of commodity spectacle and the establishment of an internal order of 'decorous demeanour' among workers and customers alike. The new temples and palaces extracted a discipline of deference and reverence which provides a powerful testimony to the class character of their intended audience. I noted earlier that Roy Rosenzweig (1984) recorded the process through which the new picture palaces created a more decorous climate for film watching, which involved the suppression of the communal disorderliness associated with the nickelodeon. A similar story could also be told about the department stores, featuring the carefully modulated demeanour of the discreetly uniformed sales staff and the regulatory roles of doormen, floorwalkers and the like. The world of spectacle, fantasy and 'consuming passions' was supported and sustained by careful stage management.

These new systems of distribution and exchange affected patterns of consumption. In tracing these, it is useful to distinguish between the public and private forms which consumption can take, and to consider how the rise of mass consumption has affected both forms of consumption and the relations between them, since the boundary between public and private is in no sense a stable one. Even at the turn of the century much domestic consumption continued to involve a large amount of domestic production, particularly, in terms of food and clothing. Such production-for-domestic-consumption, together with the provision of domestic care, was a central element of the woman's role in the home. The raw materials of such domestic production would be supplemented by both bartering and the purchase of commodities (through highly localized *petit bourgeois* patterns of trading and distribution). Such networks of shopping and shopkeeping meant the existence of a commercial infrastructure to support localized variants of class–ethnic cultures, supplying distinctive foodstuffs, reading matter, religious goods, and so forth.

The public realm of consumption also involved the intersection of familial, communal and commercial practices and relationships in terms of the use of public spaces (family outings, street cultures, clubs and societies) and the uses of localized commercial facilities (bars, eating places, music halls, nickelodeons, and so on). Again, the local nature of such provision meant it was more likely to be responsive to the prevailing class and ethnic composition of the neighbourhood. In this sense, the growth of mass consumption is not the emergence of patterns of commercial consumption into non-commercial, pre-capitalist cultural forms. No pure cultural communities existed, separate from the market-place. The impact of mass consumption lay precisely in its ability to transform the existing networks of domestic, communal and commercial consumption. Its initial invasion of the processes of working-class consumption was not founded on the invention of new needs, but on shifting the servicing of existing needs into new structures of production, distribution and exchange. In the provision of food, drink, clothing and entertainment the crucial change was to new forms of supply for existing needs, to bring domestic and communal processes more fully into market relations of exchange, and to begin the integration of *petit bourgeois* trading into systematic retailing.

This rise of a Fordist system of mass consumption reworked the processes of both domestic and public consumption. It undercut the pattern of household production, changing the character of domestic labour (though not its gender specificity), moving it from food production to shopping and food preparation, for example.[4] At the same time, the change in domestic labour coincides with the effort to reorganize the landscape and meaning of the home – with the spread of interior design, mass produced furniture, and the earliest forms of mass produced home entertainment (the radio and phonograph.) Labour saving devices and a domestic economy increasingly based on commodity purchase rather than domestic production – coincided with the intensificiation of the domestic labour of cleaning, cooking and home-making as the home itself came to be invested with greater symbolic significance.

In different ways, the main features of public consumption were also transformed through economic and political processes. The *petit bourgeois* service sector of small traders was increasingly subordinated to, and marginalized by, the corporate structures of department and chain stores, mirrored in the incorporation of sport and the entertainment industry as mass distributed forms of leisure. Public space itself was subjected to increasing regulation. Those areas which had provided free spaces as focal points for working-class cultural practices – the bars and the streets – were more tightly controlled to make them 'safe' places for respectable pursuits (see Peiss, 1986, on the work of the 'vice squads' and moral reformers).

The overall effect of these changes was less the construction of a culture of consumption than the large scale reworking of the infrastructure within which consumption is located. This expansion of the market undermined and marginalized the previous customary institutional arrangements which had supported localized forms of popular culture. The universalizing tendency of the market had two different, though related, aspects. On the one hand, there was the tendency towards 'economic universality', identified by Braverman: the subjection of increasing areas of social life to market relations. On the other hand, there was also a tendency towards cultural universalization: to standardize and nationalize the content of what the market supplies. Localized forms are in this sense undermined economically (by the emergence of national corporate producers and suppliers) and marginalized culturally (as a national-popular culture is created).

The most obvious point about these transformations of consumption concerns the way in which they have made the practice of consumption increasingly dependent on the cash-nexus. The price has to be paid to gain entry to either the public or private palaces of pleasure. Consequently, access to the universal market remains profoundly uneven in distribution. It is one aspect where there is no universalizing tendency. Historically, as Davis (1986) argues, Fordism was a process which integrated the core working class through the high wage economy into the promises and pleasures of consumption. The fact that these core sections were predominantly male and white is not without interest, since it determined the shape of the culture of consumption which followed. The structuring of the working class by race and gender meant that unequal conditions of access to consumption existed from the outset. Even where women had relatively privileged access (via a high male 'family wage'), such access was always problematic because of the internal family tensions over the allocation and use of the male wage. William Leach (1984), for example, suggests that the new credit facilities of the department stores provided a source of family conflict, since women shoppers were freed from the confines of the available housekeeping money and shopped outside of their husbands' control.

It is important to remember how class specific the emergence of the universal market was in the early decades of the twentieth century. The department stores, for example, did not immediately offer themselves as a 'democracy of images', but provided a new form of class constituted decorum. They created an exclusivity of consumption which both in its manner and its real conditions of access (cash and credit) closed its doors to the 'great unwashed'. It may be that the windows of such stores changed the face of the city for the working class, but their relation to the contents of such stores was that of window shopping. Mass production for the working-class market remained

basically functional, and outside the realms of taste and conspicuous consumption, since such practices required a disposable
income not available to most members of the working class (the
exceptions being the unmarried working young: Peiss 1986).

The unlocking of the old moral economy of the middle classes,
traced by Lears (1983), to permit them to consume was coinci-
dent with continuing attempts to moralize the working class:
to instil precisely those habits of sobriety, thrift, respectability
and orderliness which had characterized respectable middle-class
America. One does not need a theory of cultural schizophrenia,
or even middle-class hypocrisy, to account for the class specific
insistence on consumption as the reward for wealth on the one
hand, and the need for the poor to be soberly diligent on
the other.[5] To have access to the democracy of commodities,
after all, workers first needed to learn how to work. While the
middle class was learning how to enjoy itself, the working class
was being subjected to public and private initiatives aimed at
reforming its disorderliness – a disorderliness which involved
some forms of overconsumption: of alcohol, in particular.

Class played a further role in the formation of the new
consumer culture. Both Lears and the Ewens emphasize how
the emergent culture of consumption drew part of its cultural
dynamic from the forms and content of popular cultures. Kathy
Peiss has highlighted the role played by working-class cultures
in the formation of the new mass culture of the early twentieth
century, for example, in the remaking of Coney Island as a
entertainment centre:

> Thus Coney Island exemplifies not only the decline of a
> genteel middle class cultural hegemony . . . but the rise of a
> heterosocial culture that owed its form in part to the structure
> of working class social life . . . These changes grew out
> of the commercial transformations of popular amusements,
> including those of a new middle class that gloried in the
> midway and rejected genteel culture. Just as significant to
> this development, however, were the popular amusements
> of working-class youth. In Coney Island's Bowery they rec-
> ognised their street life, in the dance halls and variety shows
> familiar customs and behaviour, and in the new amusement
> parks the celebration of sexuality and romance that was so

much a part of youthful social life. Amusement park owners adopted these cultural forms and tamed them for a new mass audience that was more responsive to an expressive, heterosocial culture. (1986: 137–8.)

The cultural sources for middle-class consumption were diverse – drawing on the symbolism of European decadence (especially in fashion), domesticating the exotic imagery of the Orient and so on. But one central role was played by the appropriation and reworking of elements from the indigenous popular culture. Such elements had to be made respectable in this process of appropriation, but the formation of the culture of consumption rested heavily on such appropriations, whose best-known (and still most striking) example is the recurrent revitalization of popular music through the appropriation of black musical forms (Chambers 1985).

As a consequence, when the expansion of mass consumption beyond its original middle-class horizons took place, the new consumers of the working class found themselves confronted by a culture in which they were already in place. Their entry to mass consumption was not to an alien culture, but to one in which many of the cultural forms and symbols invited them to recognize (or 'misrecognize') themselves. These forms of what Stuart Hall (1981) has called 'cultural ventriloquism' need to be viewed alongside the simultaneous destruction of pre-existing forms of popular cultural practice and their communal infrastructures. The revitalization and expansion of mass consumption has involved a constant – and constantly speeded up – search for new vernaculars and increasing invasions of black cultures, deviant subcultures, and social movements of opposition and protest to provide the next shock of the new.

These arguments suggest that the insertion of subordinate social groups into the culture of consumption is more complex than a pessimistic reading of the destruction of popular forms and the erection of a bourgeois hegemony would allow. At the same time, they open up questions about the nature of the consumer identity which is created at the heart of these patterns of mass consumption.

SHOPPING FOR YOURSELF:
THE PRODUCTION OF THE CONSUMER

At the heart of critical analyses of mass consumption lies an argument about the dominance of the consumer as the major social identity or role: the creation of social subjects who define themselves by what they consume and through their position in the exchange relationships of the market. The construction of this identity as the dominant form of social subjectivity involved the destruction or displacement of earlier (and potentially oppositional) forms of social identity based upon class/ethnic social positions. Such identities were decomposed in the insertion of subordinate social groups into the massifying and Americanizing process of consumption, such that the sense of self comes to be validated only through the act of market mediated consumption:

> The acceptable arena of human initiative is circumscribed by the act of purchasing, given the status of consumer or audience. Within the logic of consumer imagery, the source of creative power is the object world, invested with the subjective power of 'personality' ... Consumerism engendered passivity and conformity within this supposedly ever-expanding realm of the new, which put leisure, beauty and pleasure in the reach of all. Customary bonds of affection and interdependence, born of other circumstances, disintegrated. (Ewen and Ewen, 1982: 75.)

The attention given to this dominant identity has, however, marginalized any consideration of how this role is articulated within other social identities. The exploration of the consumer has presumed the destruction of other identities, rather than considering their reconstruction around consumption. In spite of the complex analyses of the consumption which are presented in the book edited by Fox and Lears (1983), one central relationship – that of waged work and consumption – is left untouched. Loosening the bonds of ascetic Protestantism to allow the middle class to consume involved not just the creation of the mental or psychological propensity to consume, but also required a reconstruction of the significance of work –

crudely, to instrumentalize it as the condition of access to consumption, as opposed to its supposedly inherently satisfying or vocational character in the Protestant vision. Waged work was instrumentally subordinated to the new ends that it could serve – the fulfilment of the self in leisure time and through consumption.

This suggests that the hegemony of the consumer identity rests less upon the wholesale destruction of other social identities, and more on their increasing subordination to, and articulation with, the central symbolic figure of the consumer. Consumption depends upon the ideological and motivational reconstruction of The Worker (in all its differentiated forms) to link together the Fordist ensemble of labour, income and the rewards of consumption. Equally, it is dependent upon the re-articulation of The Home and the role of The Wife. The (ideal) female role for the middle-class woman in the early twentieth century had to be reworked from that of 'household manager' into the 'rational consumer' of and for the family (Wilson 1983). As wives and mothers, women were to stand at the intersection of the household economy and the consumer market-place: shopping became the quintessentially female activity. Maxine Seller notes how immigrant women being taught English learnt their role as consumers: 'Men learned to read such signs as EXIT and FIRE ALARM; women learned to read signs such as BARGAIN SALE and REDUCED. (1982: 24.) These new articulations were most powerfully expressed in the rhetorics of advertising: the perfect home composed by the housewife-shopper; the perfect child-rearing environment demonstrated by the possession of appropriate toys, clothes, nappies, and so on.

Historically, the primary social identification of the consumer is *familial*, through the wife/mother as the rational consumer. This is the core sector – and the core identity – for the expansion of mass consumption. It represents the opening up of the domestic economy (and the social relations of domesticity) to the universal market. The hegemony of consumption needs to be viewed through this nodal point. The family became the key nexus of the social relations of advanced capitalism: the integrating force in the relations of production and consumption. Ideally, the family provided the ideological/psychological motivation for (male) waged labour which supported patterns of consumption organized by (female) unpaid domestic labour. The family was also the site of the emotional or psychic investment in those labour processes – both for present satisfactions and future possibilities (Clarke and Critcher 1985, 164–175). Equally, the exceptions to this process of domesticated consumption have tended to be defined by their positions within familial relations. Consumption outside the family has tended to be the privilege of two groups: adult males and adolescents. Adult males claimed the wage earner's 'right' to forms of collective consumption outside of the home (sports, drinking and so forth); while the semi-autonomous (although gender differentiated) status of adolescents, often underpinned by relatively high levels of disposable income, has permitted involvement in non-familial cultures (Peiss 1986).

In this process of linking consumption to the domestic economy, the family was itself reconstructed. Mass consumption meant the thorough-going invasion of the private space of the family by the public realm of the market: aiming to intensify and validate the private pleasures of the Home. Women's domestic role was reconstructed: their function becoming that of transforming the family income into the materials needed to fulfil the family's wants. In the process, new forms of domestic labour were substituted for the old. Much of what mass consumption offered was the commercial provision of goods and services previously produced within the domestic economy ('convenience' foods supplanting food production and preservation; ready made clothes in place of sewing and knitting; laundries or washing machines in place of hand washing, and so on). Not all of the old labours disappeared, of course, but acquired a more subordinate (and to some extent culturally denigrated) place alongside the new skills of consumption. What the growth of mass consumption achieved was to place the family at the centre of Fordism – linking the family wage to the family shopping.

All of these processes have been extensively discussed else-where, but I have two reasons for pursuing this argument about the articulation rather than the destruction of other social identities. On the one hand, the view of consumption as an ensemble of articulated identities allows the exploration of the potential tensions within that ensemble, such that there may be a less than perfect meshing of the consumer role with other social identities. On the other hand, thinking of consumption as taking place through an ensemble of social identities raises the issue of the social and cultural conditions of consumption as an active cultural practice, informed by the other social identities in the ensemble.

DUPES AND GUERILLAS: THE DIALECTICS OF CULTURAL CONSUMPTION

At the centre of any analysis of the contradictory place of consumption in modern capitalist societies must be a grasp of the economic relations and processes within which consumption is located. This is not to argue that these economic processes exhaust all the aspects of consumption, but that to separate practices of consumption from these relations means missing crucial dynamics in the way it is shaped. In this context, I want to do no more than to outline the elementary economic forms which underlie the development of mass consumption.

First and foremost are the generic economic tendencies of capitalism towards the concentration of economic power: in the form of highly diversified multi-national corporations. These forms are the dominant ones in the field of consumption, encompassing production, distribution and exchange in the provision of food, clothing, entertainment, etc. (Clarke and Critcher 1985, Chapter 3). Such concentrations of economic power are not directly reflected in processes of cultural massification or uniformity. On the contrary economic concentration has coexisted with increasing diversity in terms of the objects and services produced for consumption. This mixture of concentration and diversity has a number of different aspects. One is the status of diversity as the residue of the process of concentration (take-overs, and mergers), leaving behind distinctive brand names, titles and consumer loyalties. These may constitute a set of 'traditions' which may be maintained precisely for the appearance of diversity which they sustain (the car industry and brewing exhibit these tendencies). Such in-house diversity has been enhanced by the development of new production technologies which enable a range of carefully differentiated products to be delivered from the same production process. At the point of distribution, such production based diversification is mirrored in what Bluestone *et al.*(1981) have identified as the 'speciality store' within the department store: the internal fragmentation of the store into separate shops corresponding to brand names, designer labels, and so forth.

A second aspect of diversity in consumption derives from the self-consciously cultural, or aesthetic, character of many of the products of consumer culture (design, music, entertainment, and so on). These processes, in what might be termed the 'cultural industries', often involve a relationship between corporate production and distribution and processes of semi-autonomous or petty commodity production. Music, film and television provide primary examples of this interlocking of the 'creative labour' of cultural production, where creativity is bought in or contracted out, and the corporate structures of mass reproduction and distribution. One distinctive effect of these complex structures of cultural production is the maintenance of a material basis for ideologies of creativity. While it is true that the production of new (or even novel) cultural objects is dependent on sources of creative labour, the material relations of cultural production and distribution are happily ignored in favour of a celebration of creative freedom (for example 'editorial freedom'), thus losing sight of the structuring powers of corporate capital ranging from agenda setting and selectivity through to direct censorship.

The other economic force which works to maintain diversity in the market-place is the continuing (though changed) role of the *petit bourgeoisie* in production and distribution. Traditionally, there has been a strong *petit bourgeois* role in the distributive and service sectors, often servicing distinctive ethinc-cultural needs, marginalized by the Americanizing uniformity of the mass market. The revival of cultural ethnicity in the last twenty years, allied to a more cosmopolitan culture among the professional and managerial classes, has given such cultural diversity a much more visible presence in the culture of consumption. Intersecting with these developments is the post 'countercultural' revival of arts and crafts in handicraft manufacture of clothing, jewellery, furnishings, and so forth. In addition, and perhaps the most distinctive innovation in the *petit bourgeois* sector, there are the implications of some of the new information technologies which have allowed the development of so-called 'garage industries' in such fields as computer software, video-making, and music production. Such developments feed the constant revitalization of cultural production both within the *petit bourgeois* sector and through their potential incorporation into the corporate cultural industries.

These expansionary tendencies of the culture of consumption undercut the assumptions of 'cultural pessimism' about the unity of economic interests and ideological domination. The pessimistic view of the incorporation of passive subordinate groups into a bourgeois hegemony through the process of consumption fails to take account of the contradictions that the creation and constant recreation of a popular culture involves. The economic impulse of the culture of consumption, its search for new markets and profits, has always involved the revitalization of popular culture through the use of subordinate, oppositional and alternative cultural forms and practices. This poses a tension between the logic of the economic impulse and the ideological drive towards hegemony: innovation versus conventionalization. The cultural industries need to be seen both as exploratory and responsive (to social and cultural changes) and as conventionalizing and containing (reconciling the new to existing cultural expectations).

This process of cultural revitalization can be characterized as 'the appropriation of the vernacular': expansion through the use of pre-existing popular or subordinate culture. It raises a number of problems about the relationship between hegemony and popular culture. First, it means that it is important to recognize that hegemony is not a process of supplanting an 'indigenous' or 'authentic' popular culture by the imposition of an 'alien' or 'bourgeois' culture. Rather, it is the creation of a national-popular culture which reworks popular forms and content through a process of translation into the themes, forms and conventions of hegemony. To put it metaphorically, we might view the passage of the popular/vernacular elements into a national-popular culture as a process which requires popular forms to lose their rough edges, to become 'respectable' and capable of being generalized well beyond their points of origin.

Unless we subscribe to a view of culture that distinguishes between 'authentic' and 'false' cultural symbols, the significance of this appropriation of 'vernacular forms' for analysing popular culture is considerable. Most importantly, it suggests that we should view the cultural content of mass consumption not as the product or effect of a 'bourgeois culture' or ideology, but as a highly contradictory *ensemble* of diverse cultural elements.[6] This includes appropriations from the cultures of subordinate groups, which find themselves nationalized (and in some cases, internationalized) beyond their local origins. Dashiell Hammett, and the genre of hard-boiled writing, offer a very sharp example of this process in which the vernacular is used to revitalize cultural production, at one and the same time opening up the world of the vernacular to a respectable readership, and also making reading a practice of consumption for a wider audience, undermining its cultural exclusivity. It is important to remember that, as Peiss argues, this process is one of transformation rather than reproduction – things happen to the vernacular in the process of appropriation. The original popular forms may be 'cleaned up' (as in the lyrics of 'Rock around the Clock'), sanitized, or sentimentalized (as in many instances of populism in the American film), but even allowing for such changes, what is at stake is the use of popular forms to sustain the cultural content of mass production and consumption.

These arguments may seem to sustain the conclusions of the 'cultural pessimists': an absence of authenticity, the power of cultural ventriloquism, and a popular culture saturated in hegemonic connections. But that would be to stop the dialectics of cultural production and consumption before they are complete. Once again, it would mean returning to a view of consumption which sees people only as consumers – linked only to a mediated national-popular culture. However we are always more than consumers, always located in other sets of social relations and social identities (of class, gender, race, age, locality, and so on). Each of these carries with it a series of cultural practices and resources with which the national-popular culture strives to intersect, by addressing us and inviting us to recognize ourselves in its imagery. But the emphasis here must be placed on the words 'strives to', rather than presuming that such addresses and intersections are monolithically successful. Indeed, many of the struggles of cultural politics over the last twenty years, concerning the representations in the popular media of gender,

race, sexuality, and disability, for example, point precisely to the
failure of the national-popular to construct such intersections.

To this needs to be added a consideration of the polysemic
character of signs: their ability to carry more than one meaning,
and thus to be available for different readings. (A character
perfectly expressed in the diverse readings of Bruce Springsteen's
track 'Born in the USA', which has been read as both celebratory
and condemnatory of the contemporary state of the nation.) This
potential diversity of meaning in the sign allied to the differentiated social positions in which consumers are socially located
suggests that the 'insertion' of consumers into the hegemonic
domain of a national-popular culture is profoundly uneven.
Signs may be absorbed according to their stabilized (preferred or
dominant meaning), that is, consumers may behave like the ideal
consumer. Signs may be appropriated partially or selectively;
treated ironically, or with indifference or hostility. They may
also be reworked, transposed and have alternative meanings
imposed on them. Cora Kaplan has argued this in relation to
the consumption of the American soap opera *Dallas*:

> *Dallas* may, in part, be pleasurable to watch not because the
> fantasy it engenders fulfils our most unprogressive social and
> psychic desires, but rather because it allows us to make fun
> of them. Which is surely one way its makers intend it to grab
> us. Most of the mass popular narrative made today for an
> international viewing or reading audience has a deliberately
> ambiguous, even unstable tone. Enjoy it as melodrama or as
> satire, *or both*, the texts seem to say. Make it part of whatever
> political paradigm you like, only enjoy.
>
> Yet that instability of tone exposes, deliberately again, the
> narrative conventions, encouraging viewers of all kinds to dis-
> cuss the form and limits of serial soap as part of the pleasure
> of consumption. This self-aware element of soaps does not
> make the product radical, but it does tend to make its effects
> quite complicated and contradictory, harder to pin down for
> all or every class, gender, age and race of viewer. Into that
> gap between plot and presentation . . . the social and political
> context in which *Dallas* is seen by different cultural, class and
> national constituencies is inserted, and determines how it will,
> in the end, be understood. (1986: 39; emphasis in original.)

It is this 'field of possibilities' that constitutes cultural consumption as a social and cultural practice – as opposed to seeing
it collapsed into the economic and ideological domination of
the exchange relationship. It is also the idea of active cultural
practice which cultural studies in its varied forms has sought
to stress: the bending of received cultures to a role in a 'lived'
cultural project; the making sense of the social relations which
people inhabit, and the construction of cultural strategies for
surviving those processes. Even so, there are some difficulties
surrounding these arguments.

One problem is that the types of readings of popular culture
offered by Kaplan and others have tended towards a radical
culturalism, emphasizing the volatility of meaning at the expense
of two other considerations. On the one hand, the emphasis on
volatility of meaning has displaced a concern with the economic
conditions of cultural production and consumption. Like the
'resistances' which they analyse, many of the studies of the
cultural creativity of consumers tend to take the conditions
of production and exchange for granted, leaving them as the
unexamined background to the cultural projects of subordinated
groups. In that sense, these approaches miss the structured
secondariness of consumption. On the other hand, this disconnection of cultural texts from their conditions of production
is reflected in the overestimation of the polysemic character
of the sign. While signs may carry multiple meanings, their
insertion into the field of hegemony also involves efforts to
fix or stabilize preferred or dominant meanings: to inflect the
sign in one particular direction. This suggests that reading (that
is the signifying practice of consumption) is not a free floating
process, but a process of cultural struggle in which alternative or
oppositional meanings have to be worked for and won against
hegemonic meanings (Ellsworth 1988).

It is also important to register the cultural, as well as economic,
limitations on this relativization of meaning. It is not sufficient
to point to the existence of social difference (as Kaplan does)
as the basis for cultural diversity: positions of social difference
merely constitute the possibility of cultural diversity, and do not
guarantee its realization. The creation of alternative meanings
requires the use of alternative cultural resources: vocabularies of
difference that can articulate social divisions. One of the effects

of a nationalising popular culture may be to rework positions
of social division and antagonism as mere difference, and to
circumscribe vocabularies of division (as in the naturalization
of gender divisions, for example).

A further difficulty is how to avoid romanticizing the political
character of cultural resistances. While this approach correctly
gets rid of the pessimism of seeing subordinate groups as 'cultural
dupes', the alternative vision of guerilla armies of cultural activists seems excessively celebratory, and contains few means for
assessing the political direction of such resistances. A variety of
subcultural studies have revealed – either implicitly or explicitly
– the potentially regressive character of resistance, constructing
cultural projects which have as their dynamics the reproduction
of the 'bad sense' of 'common sense': its racism, its sexism or
its homophobia (for example, Hall and Jefferson, eds. 1976 and
Willis 1979). Since the social positions and relations on which
they rest are contradictory and potentially antagonistic, splitting
the social subject through race, class, gender and other social
identities, there is no guarantee that cultural diversity does not
reproduce or reinforce these divisions.

The distance which social divisions may create between cultural commodities and their consumption can also take the form
of cynicism. Although the repertoire of cynicism ('well, they
would say that, wouldn't they?' or 'you can't take it seriously')
involves a form of refusal, it is nevertheless demobilizing: a state
of *passive* dissent. The playfulness of postmodernism evokes
precisely this state of emotional and/or political disinvestment:
a refusal to be engaged (see Grossberg 1989). There is, then,
nothing intrinsic in the practice of alternative readings that
requires them to promote the forging of larger collective identities of opposition. The dilemmas of the split between structural
pessimism and cultural radicalism are nowhere more sharply
visible than in responses to the changing shape of consumption
in the 1980s.

AFTER THE MASS?

For the most part, the various analyses of cultural consumption which I have been talking about assume the structure of

Fordism as the established basis of metropolitan economies of mass consumption. But there are now arguments which suggest that Fordism may no longer be either a stable or a dominant economic formation in the USA (for example, Davis 1986). Fordism was a formation which linked the high-wage economy to the continuous enlargement of mass consumption, mediated by the sexual division of labour within the family (and formed a basis for linkages between organized labour, corporate capital and the state in the process). One consequence of Fordism was to distinguish the core metropolitan economies from the peripheral low-wage economies in the period of postwar imperialism. But Fordism also constructed core and periphery within the metro- politan societies: geographically, in terms of the uneven develop- ment of different regions; and socially in terms of sectoral labour markets distinguishing core labour from the marginalized (and predominantly black and female) low wage sectors.

Such distinctions intersect with the political and cultural formations of the USA, most visibly in the form of a black sub-proletariat managed by a judicious mixture of welfare and repression in the inner cities; and female labour positioned by the patriarchal economy of the family wage. These same political and cultural formations highlight the dangers of taking Fordism to refer to a whole social formation, rather than as denoting a specific combination of economic processes and relationships.[7] Within the Fordist period, the cultural formation of the USA, the processes of political representation and the form of the state have undergone substantial transformations. Such changes underline the difficulties of trying to trace direct alignments between the economic formation and the terrains of culture and politics.

In particular, the varied political and cultural struggles of the 1960s and 70s – civil rights, the women's movement, gay liberation, the counter culture, and so on – brought about significant changes in the politics and culture of a society still economically dominated by Fordism. Legal and political changes expanded some of the membership rights of marginalized and subordinated groups, changing the conditions of access to public goods as well as the private pleasures of consumption. And, to some extent, those struggles were represented in the changing composition of the national-popular culture: a more expansive presence of black cultural forms; changing representations of women's roles and sexuality; and a massive expansion of the youth market with implications for all the popular media and popular taste.

The postwar development of Fordism was articulated with an expanded corporatist state, at whose centre was a particular economic and political settlement between organized labour and 'big capital' (see, for example, Lipsitz 1982; Milton 1982, chapter 8). The contemporary crisis of Fordism and its systemic inability to overcome declining profitability has been accompanied by a crisis in corporatist politics. The postwar settlement has been the target both of the changing imperatives of US capital and the political initiatives of the New Right. (The political changes will be dealt with more extensively in the next chapter.) The increasing volatility of capital has turned some of its previously international strategies towards the domestic manufacturing sector in the US in search of further advantages from non-unionized and low-waged labour: moving manufacturing overseas, closing domestic plants or moving them to non-unionized labour areas within the US. At the same time, there have been sectoral shifts away from the traditional core sections of manufacturing into the new sunrise industries, dominated by oil and new technology as well as the secular movement from manufacturing to service sector investment and development (Davis 1986). Such a massive recomposition of capital required a recomposition of labour, in particular the destruction of the old core sections of unionized manufacturing labour which stood at the juncture of Fordism and corporatism. One major effect of this recomposition is a tendency towards a more sharply delineated 'dual labour market', with a growing separation of professional, managerial and scientific labour (as the high wage dominant sector) from an increasingly de-skilled, non-unionised, low-waged and often part-time secondary labour force (Bluestone and Harrison 1982).

Such developments have very powerful implications for the culture of consumption, most evidently in the way they affect the basic conditions of access to the pleasures of consumption – the wage. The expansion of a low-wage sector (and expanded unemployment) means a greater section of the population has come to occupy a marginal position in the cultural market-place, less able to pay the price of entry to the ever expanding possibilities of consumption, despite the fact that their employment may well be in the form of servicing 'other people's pleasure'. At the same time, however, the expanded professional and managerial classes have sustained – and indeed have driven – a massive expansion of consumption and its cultural horizons. They are the 'other people' whose pleasures need to be serviced. In their study of the retail sector, Bluestone *et al.* (1981), argue that there is evidence of a 'dual strategy' in the organization of retailing: on the one hand, there has been a massive growth of 'discount chains', aiming at marketing low-cost products with a high turnover (for example, K-Mart); while on the other, there has been a process of 'trading up' in which 'specialty' shops and chains aim to cater for more affluent and specialized 'taste'. These two tendencies may be a mirror – at the point of distribution – of the growing division of the labour market, replicating income differences in a split between quantity and quality retailing.

The most active force in the reshaping of popular culture and consumption is this expanded professional and managerial fraction of the middle class (sometimes referred to as the service class), which has inherited the role of national cultural leadership from the traditional middle classes, whose 'respectability' is now both scandalized and marginalized. As I argued in the preceding chapter, this leadership role is composed of a number of elements: the self-confidence of a class which occupies the primary subaltern positions of advanced capitalism; its high levels of disposable income, subsidised by changes in tax policies, and its historically specific (conjunctural) self-consciousness about culture and consumption.[8]

This class is marked by its relationship to the cultural inheritance from the 1960s and 70s, particularly in terms of the consequences of 'cultural politics' and 'lifestyle politics' from the diverse fields of the women's movement, the gay movement, black struggles and the counter-culture. Such cultural politics brought issues of identity and lifestyle to centre stage, and, in doing so, reworked some of the parameters of the national-popular culture. This loosening of the boundaries of the national-popular – disarticulating the 'normality' of white, male-dominated, middle-class America – also had the effect of throwing off some of the inhibitions of taste and style embedded in that culture, making a whole new set of cultural resources available for consumption. The new middle class has generated an intensified commitment to consuming style, and has increased the volatility of fashion and taste. Its economic, social and geographical mobility as a class is mirrored in its cultural mobility. Socially dislocated, it has invested heavily in cultural dislocation: the constant re-creation of style. It is culturally libertarian: disruptive of conventionality and, at the cultural level, it is also internationalist: open to the discovery of new sources of difference from Japanese food through to South African music. Its internationalism might also be read as a new cultural imperialism – the appropriation of subordinate vernaculars to provide the exotica for the consuming passions of metropolitan societies.

This cultural libertarianism is allied to a high degree of self-consciousness about the cultural practices of consumption. This self-consciousness is also generational in two closely related senses. On the one hand, this particular class fraction is shaped by the legacy of youth subcultures and their emphatic stylishness on popular culture. The diversification of music, dress, dance, and language remains a dominant force in popular culture from these origins, and generationally, the professional and middle classes have inherited some of the skills of cultural practice from that period. This is closely allied to the wider cultural inheritance of skills from postwar popular culture (captured in such phrases as 'the TV generation', and best expressed in the 'Baby Boomer' edition of *Trivial Pursuit*). It is this class/generation formation that has acquired both the knowledge of popular cultural codes and conventions, and the economic and cultural space in which to 'play' with them (and who can spot all the generic references in *Moonlighting*). This knowledge and playfulness is an essential component of this cosmopolitan popular culture, encompassing a variety of postmodern cultural practices – the apparently random or discordant juxtaposition of signs, ironic self-referencing, playing with conventions and genres, an indifference to authenticity, a celebration of camp and the subversion of conventionality. This is the social core of the idea of the knowing consumer of popular culture.

This class and generational intersection has paradoxical consequences for the contemporary culture of consumption which relate to the cultural effects of the emergence of youth culture in the 1960s and its dislocation of the conventional processes of ageing. Here the gap between the traditional and the cosmopolitan middle classes is at its sharpest, for the new professional and managerial class has refused to grow old gracefully along the traditionally expected cultural paths. Instead, it has disrupted the expected progression to respectability (the expectation that 'youth is a phase they'll grow out of'), and substituted the maintenance of youthfulness in terms of taste, style and appearance. Central to this has been the massive growth of body maintenance, both as an attempted inhibition of some of the biological processes conventionally associated with ageing, and as a set of stylistic images of youthful self-presentation.[9]

The other distinctive conjunctural feature of this new culture of consumption is its post-feminist character. I am aware that this is an extremely dangerous term to use, given its implication that feminist struggles have been superseded: that they are finished with, even if they have not been won. Nevertheless, it seems to me that this assumption is deeply inscribed in the heart of the new culture. It is shaped by a contradictory combination of the effects of feminism's successes (however partial), its existence as a political and cultural force and the belief that it has now been transcended. In spite of all the evidence of the stubborn resistance of gender inequalities to change in both public and private spheres, the new cosmopolitanism presents itself as an equal opportunities culture. It has learnt the rhetorics of gender relations and now pronounces men and women as having equal rights to consume and create lifestyles as autonomous individuals. The culture is marked by the higher profile of women, particularly in entrepreneurial, managerial and professional roles, and their representation, in diverse ways, as being liberated from the overarching identification of consumption with the home. This captures part of the new cosmopolitanism's post-feminist sensibility, in the way that it has taken up feminism's insistence on the socially constructed nature of gender identities and the plasticity of sexuality. The consequences of this view of constructed identities has, if anything, been more far reaching for the forms of masculinity,

which has become polyvalent. We have seen a proliferation of
ways of 'being a man': running the gamut from old to new.
In the process, consumption has been masculinized: opened
as an acceptable route to self-production and self-fulfilment
for men. These developments embody the paradox of a post-
feminist world in their dislocation of the plasticity of identities
from the material conditions of gender divisions. At the same
time, they underwrite the promise of guilt free ways of living in
these new identities through the post-feminist declaration that
the battle is over.

In many ways, this new cosmopolitan culture intensifies all
the political tensions and contradictions of a culture of consumption, exhibiting the extremes of optimistic and pessimistic
evaluations of popular culture. Negatively, it can be viewed
as a highly class-specific variety of conspicuous consumption,
qualitatively different only in so far as it no longer needs
to see its consumer durables as durable. Its economic and
psychological investment in the increasing volatility of style
merely reflect the conditions of economic volatility of world
capital. Similarly, its narcissistic obsession with lifestyle can be
seen as parasitic upon the accomplishments of earlier struggles
of cultural politics – now depoliticized and turned into 'radical
chic'. Such parasitism also extends to its relationship to other
subordinate cultural forms, both domestic and international, so
that listening to Paul Simon's *Graceland* is the closest connection
to the politics of South Africa. Its own creativity is limited to
the pastiche and re-treads characteristic of postmodernism. The
end result is a decadent and depoliticized cultural retreat from
the realities of advanced capitalism: a cultural libertinism rather
than a political libertarianism, cushioned by the high rewards of
service to capital.

However, all of these tendencies can also be given a positive
inflection which celebrates the creative and expansionary quality of this cultural cosmopolitanism. In refusing the passivity
ascribed to the consumer, it celebrates diversity and refuses to
close the gap between style and identity. Its playfulness with
cultural signs refuses the weight of tradition and conventionality. It creates and expands possibilities of difference rather
than foreclosing them. Its cultural libertarianism valorizes those
dimensions of personal choice which were central to cultural

politics, and is resistant to attempts to revive 'traditional morality'. Equally, its internationalism has real consequences, creating resistances to narrowly conceived nationalism and even being the source of innovation in cultural politics (USA for Africa, Live Aid, and so on). In all these directions, cultural cosmopolitanism can be seen as expansive, making new cultural and political connections possible.

By themselves, neither view of this cosmopolitan culture provides an adequate judgement, because each gives a one-sided interpretation to a highly contradictory cultural formation. The political implications of the new consumer culture are problematic, because this culture is not a simple or monolithic entity. But which of the tendencies in this culture becomes its predominant direction – whether the progressive or regressive face emerges as its driving force – is not solely a cultural matter. Rather, the outcome depends on the linkages – the articulations – between the cultural and the economic and political conditions of social life. Whether its expansiveness can be matched by an expansion of the economic and cultural conditions of popular participation, extended to those who do not have a niche of their own; whether it depoliticizes lifestyle and settles for an economic rather than political libertarianism or provides the conditions for a more emancipatory cultural politics by being connected to new political forces; and whether its internationalism can resist being a consuming imperialism are the problems of this new cosmopolitan culture. Their solution depends on the forms of articulation which are constructed between popular culture and political culture.

NOTES

The development of this chapter has been helped by conversations and correspondence with Leslie Roman, Larry Grossberg, Dick Butsch, Paul du Gay, and Janet Newman.

1   The concern with commodity fetishism is more explicit in analyses which consider the 'enhanced' cycle of fetishism associated with advertising, for example, Ewen (1976) and Jhall *et al.* (1985).
2   These studies have been criticized on a variety of grounds, some of which are relevant to the argument here. First, by focusing on

distinctive subcultural groupings or by relying on ethnogaphic studies of small groups of youth, they have been criticized for generalizing from marginal or deviant youth experiences, and thus neglecting the cultures of mainstream youth in which the cultural processes of conformity might be expected to be more highly developed. Secondly, the discussion of such subcultures in terms of 'resistance' (Hall and Jefferson eds, 1976) is said to have led to an over-romanticized and over-politicized view of their significance. This criticism identifies a series of problems with the concept of resistance: (a) that it is unspecific about what is being resisted in such subcultural practice; (b) that there is no substantial political analysis of the content and direction of these resistances (thus, white male working-class subcultures of resistance may be deeply implicated in practices of sexism and racism); and (c) that it is not clear that there are any observable political consequences of these practices of resistance on which the left might build. Finally, these studies have been criticized for seeing subcultures as the product of conscious, active subjects to whom an excess of consciousness is attributed, thus neglecting the contradictory and overdetermined character of subjectivity.

3 Some of these arguments are pursued in an article about the problems of politically evaluating popular culture: Clarke, 1990.

4 Such processes are, of course, unevenly distributed – socially, culturally and geographically.

5 This touches on a recurrent tension in middle-class culture between its traditionalist and modernizing orientations, so that the middle class simultaneously appears as both the 'moral entrepreneurs' of reform and conservation (for example, around Prohibition) and the moral libertarians (of the 'smart set', and so on).

6 Stuart Hall's 'Notes on deconstructing the Popular' (1982) remains the best starting point for this sort of analysis.

7 Fordism has proved to be a particularly tempting, and particularly difficult, concept for recent analyses of contemporary capitalism. Its origins lie in Gramsci's notes on 'Americanism and Fordism' (1971), which explore the connections between an economy centred around mass production and aspects of culture and politics in the creation of the 'collective worker'. More recently, it has been used to discuss changes in labour processes (from mass production to flexible specialization) and wider shifts in the composition and accumulation strategies of capital. Both uses carry with them problems of determinist analyses (technological and economic, respectively). In particular, there appears to be a strong temptation to draw an equivalence between the economic formation of Fordism and the political form of the state (in its expanded, welfarist, interventionist, social-democratic form). This equivalence manages to combine bad history (Fordism predates the expanded state) and a functionalist view of the state (collapsing the political crisis of the expanded state into the accumulation crisis of Fordism). As Chapter 5 argues, the two are connected but are not the same. For a more general discussion of the uses and problems of Fordism, see Rustin (1989).

8   It is also the class of the intellectuals, including those who both make and study popular culture. It is therefore not particularly surprising that much recent analysis focuses on (and indeed celebrates) this new cosmopolitanism. After all, it is ours.

9   This commitment to consuming youthfulness produces a tension around youth culture itself. For, as the previous generation refuses to move on, the cultural space of youth is constrained, already occupied and owned by those who have the economic power to stay there. New youth cultural innovations are appropriated and consumed as a part of staying young, and the young themselves have to find still newer forms of being different (running the gamut from yet more extreme stylistic outrage or nihilism through to the reconstruction of ultra-conservative or ultra-respectable styles). Equally, the new cosmopolitan youthfulness has involved a consumption of its own youth, in the reworking of the imagery of 1950s and 60s youth culture (retro styles, the revival of soul music, and so on).

5
Hard times: the American New Right and welfare

The politics of the 1980s have been overshadowed by the rise of the New Right. Between them, Ronald Reagan and Margaret Thatcher have overturned two of the central assumptions which had underpinned Marxist analyses of the state during the resurgence of Marxism as a form of intellectual enquiry. During the late 1960s and 70s, the state became a primary object of study for Western Marxism. Most of the theoretical endeavour focused upon questions of state form and state function: the nature and role of the state in advanced capitalism. Analyses centred around such matters as the state's role in managing the contradictions between accumulation and legitimation; the relative autonomy of the state; the role of the state in securing the consent of subordinated classes; the ideological functions of the state, and so on.

Behind these issues stood two assumptions about the state in advanced capitalist societies. The first was that the *form* of the state was relatively stable: that what was called the 'corporatist' or 'social democratic' form of the state was the appropriate form for advanced capitalist economies. This form of capitalist state ensured (in however contradictory a fashion) that the economic and political incorporation of the subordinate classes in the Western liberal democracies, and worked to sustain the continued conditions of capital accumulation (through economic management; welfare intervention, and so on). Although the analyses of the workings of this state form are highly varied, there existed a widespread presumption that the form itself was 'the best possible shell' for the economies of the West. Alongside this stood the second assumption: that the processes of political representation were, at best, of secondary significance. The rotation of parties within the field of bipartisan 'consensus politics' were of interest in terms of the maintenance of legitimacy through political ritual, but were structurally framed by the conditions of the corporatist state.

The rise of the New Right in Britain, the USA and elsewhere has subverted these assumptions. The electoral successes of the Conservatives and Republicans in 1979 and 1980 respectively (and their subsequent repetitions) marked the re-emergence of 'ideological politics' and involved the election of governments which identified the corporatist state itself as the enemy. At the centre of these ideological politics has been an attack on the expanded state (in its various guises of liberalism, collectivism, socialism and the like), coupled with promises to 'roll it back', 'get it off the people's backs' and 'break its shackles'. One effect of these developments has been to provoke a crisis of theory on the left: an uncertainty about how to understand and evaluate these changes of direction. This uncertainty has manifested itself in a variety of wild oscillations. Here a new economism (capitalist crisis = reactionary politics) counterposed against an over politicization (in which the economic dimension is omitted in favour of a detailed study of the New Right's political organization).[1] Equally, the sophisticated analyses of the incorporative, repressive and patriarchal dimension of state intervention through its welfare apparatus have been called into question by the problems of how to defend such services and facilities for the poor when they are under attack from the right. As a variety of writers have observed, the rise of the New Right has thrown the left's ambiguous (not to say profoundly contradictory) relationship to the state into sharp relief.[2] Finally, it must also be admitted that the development of an ideological politics holds out a fatal fascination for intellectuals of the left: a reluctant admiration for the creation of an intellectually driven, ideologically self-conscious politics ('if only it was ours'). As will be clear from what follows, this fascination leads us to scour the writings and sayings of the New Right to uncover the ideological motifs, their modes of address, their discursive strategies, their thematic unities and their rhetorical power.

While such approaches have been an important counterweight to reductionist analyses of the New Right which treat them as merely the *petit bourgeois* front for the latest capitalist onslaught, there is a tendency to overstate the ideological effectivity and political accomplishments of the New Right. The development of conjunctural political analysis is a welcome addition to the left's armoury, away from the de-historicizing effects of theorizing the capitalist state, but carries with it the danger of failing to connect the conjunctural to the organic: the longer term tendencies and developments of capitalist economic, social and political formations.

What follows is an attempt to examine the conjuncture of the American New Right's political dominance, linking it to the more organic, long term, conditions of crisis within the USA, and to explore what sort of solutions the New Right has offered to the different dimensions of crisis. Within this, a more narrowly defined aim is to explore why the state's role in welfare has played such a central part in the New Right's ideological and political project.

AN AMERICAN NIGHTMARE: THE CONDITIONS OF CRISIS

The late 1970s saw an unusually self-conscious development of the collective interests of American capital (which had never been particularly modest or retiring about its own concerns). We might identify three specific tributaries feeding into this new self-consciousness: each a particular concern or fear for the future. The first concerned the impact of a world recession on both the international and domestic fortunes of American capital, ranging from energy prices to the rise of manufacturing competition around the Pacific Basin. The second and linked in complex ways to the first, was the continued internationalization of US capital, seeking to free itself from the limitations of the domestic economy and take advantage of favourable market conditions on a global scale. Paradoxically, as Bluestone and Harrison (1982) have pointed out, this internationalization meant that much of the foreign competition held responsible for the decline of domestic manufacturing was in fact owned by the same US companies busy closing their domestic plants in the face of this competition. And the third, US capital was anxious to dis-establish the corporatist solution of the 1950s and 60s: to disentangle itself from the web of connections to organized labour and the state. While the postwar settlement linking 'big capital, big labour and the state' in a high-wage consumption oriented economy had proved both productive and profitable, it now represented a fetter on the further development of capital, tying it into union agreements, plants, patterns of national and local taxation, and forms of production which were less than optimal. Capital wished to free itself from these ties in order to find new sectors, new labour forces, new markets and new sources of profitability.

The business agenda was relatively simple and straightforward: more favourable taxation; less state regulation and reducing the power of organized labour (Moody 1987). Each of these would contribute to freeing capital from the costs and limits of the corporatist settlement. This agenda was articulated through a rapid growth in the number of political organizations representing capital: the Business Roundtable and corporate Political Action Committees (PACs). Moody records that corporate PACs increased in number from 89 in 1974, to 784 in 1978, to 1467 by 1984. The amount of political funds donated by Trade Association and Corporate PACs increased from $8 million in 1972, to $84.9 million by 1982 (Moody 1987: 165–6).

This political presentation of the business agenda overlaid the processes of economic restructuring of US capital: the secular shift from manufacturing to service industries; the geographical shift from the north east to the south; the move from heavy industry to the new sunrise industries; and the accompanying recompositions of the labour force consequent upon these shifts (Bluestone and Harrison 1982; Davis 1986). These processes of economic restructuring unlocked some of the ties of the corporatist settlement, particularly in relation to organized labour. Concessionary wage settlements (especially following the Chrysler bail out in 1980) were struck, plant closures, and the shifting of production to non-unionized plants were undertaken. All these trends were under way in the late 1970s, and with consequences for the social formation of US capitalism. One consequence was the destablization of the assumptions of the high-wage economy and its promised pay offs in consumption for labour in the traditional core sectors of manufacturing.

In these ways, the elements of economic crisis (and the consequent efforts of US capital to restructure itself) can be seen as contributing to a crisis of the state form, undermining the corporatist settlement. Under increasing attack from the representatives of capital, and increasingly seen as unable to deliver its promises by core sections of the working class, the economic costs of the corporatist state were simultaneously being shifted from corporate to individual taxation (Cronin and Radtke 1987: 279–80). In this sense, the state became increasingly exposed as a political target, particularly in terms of the experience of the tax burden, pushed upwards by inflation during the years of the Carter administration. This incipient collapse of the corporatist settlement manifested itself in a variety of ways among those class strata who had been its beneficiaries: unemployment; the loss of bargaining power (over the wage, job control, plant closure, and so on); increased taxation (including property as well as personal taxation); declining access to consumption, including the promise of suburban home ownership, all combining to represent the abandonment of at least one version of the American dream (Hunter 1988a). The visible feature of this collapse was the failure of the state: the putative guarantor of the promises of the corporatist settlement. The collapse represented the failure of big government to perform its part of the partnership: that of national economic management. Economically, the Carter years combined recession, inflation, the energy crisis, rising unemployment and rising taxation.

This crisis of corporatism intersected with a further dimension of social and political crisis: the crisis of liberalism. This involves a distinction between the form of the state (corporatism) and the dominant political ideology of the period (liberalism, or, to be more precise, corporate liberalism, given the varieties of liberalism which abound). It was this variety of liberalism that provided the political ideology which guided the expansion of the state through the 1960s and 70s and which shaped the dominant political culture of the period. Thematically, this version of liberalism combines an élite commitment to the rational use of the state to reconcile the interests of the major economic blocs (corporate capital and organized labour); to promote the USA's international interests; to manage a high consumption domestic economy within a culture of expanded personal freedoms; and to manage domestic social problems. While other elements of corporate liberalism are enmeshed in the the crisis of the corporatist state, it is this last aspect – the expanded role of the state in social management – which emerged at the centre of the social and political crisis of liberalism.

Through the 1960s and 70s, the state became the focal point for the struggles of subordinate groups within American society (the Civil Rights Movement, women's movements, gay and lesbian movements and so on). The combination of these pressures on the state for judicial and social reform with a liberal political culture committed to using the state as a means of rational social reconstruction produced an expanded social, as well as economic, role for the state. The outcome was an increasingly interventionist judiciary (affirming social and political rights) together with a much expanded social welfare system. Although these are politically identified with the Kennedy/Johnson Democratic presidencies (the Great Society programmes), many of the domestic policies of an expanded state remained in place through the periods of Nixon and Ford Republicanism.

These policies reveal the contradictory qualities of corporate liberalism. Although in no way committed to the major reconstruction of social inequalities, the culture of corporate liberalism was responsive to demands for equal rights, for limited social reform, and for programmes directed towards poverty within a framework of a progressive interpretation of the liberal agenda. Within the political and economic breathing-space provided by the corporatist settlement, corporate liberalism could envisage the use of the state to promote some degree of social reconstruction and the management of social problems through expanded state intervention. The containment of new social and political movements from subordinate groups within the limits of liberalism – the agenda of individual rights and equality of access rather than class actions and the equalization of outcome – emerged as the focal point of corporate liberalism's contradictions (Eisenstein 1987). The political culture of corporate liberalism both identified the state as the object or target for social movements, and raised the expectations of subordinate groups through its commitment to an admittedly limited agenda of social and political reform. Corporate liberalism constructed the political and cultural space within which subordinate groups could present legitimate claims on the state. The effect was to create a double, and contradictory, pressure on the social direction established by corporate liberalism. On the one hand, its economic and political base lay in the corporatist settlement and its domestic agenda was driven by the commitment to a high consumption economy and culture framed by the imagery of Middle America: suburbanized home owning nuclear families surrounded by consumer durables (Hunter 1988a). On the other hand, the pressures from social movements excluded from or marginal to both the settlement and the image of the Middle American way identified as the good life created demands on the state to improve access to these desirable conditions. The effects were often the promotion of social tendencies which ran counter to the desired way of life: black culture in the heart of the white American dream, and increasing women's access to waged work when the imagery of the American family demanded a domestic and domesticated mother.

The conditions for the political emergence of the New Right were laid by the combined effect of these different dimensions of crisis: the crisis of accumulation; the collapse of the corporatist settlement; and the contradictions of corporate liberalism. Together, they seemed to constitute a state of national decay and decline: economically, socially, culturally and politically. All this was overlaid, and given emphasis, by the international weakness of the Carter administration. Even so, these conditions still needed to be turned into a coherent narrative: to tell the story of national decline and its possible solution. This was the self-appointed task of the New Right. As Gramsci has argued: 'It may be ruled out that immediate economic crises of themselves produce fundamental historical events; they can simply create a terrain more favourable to the dissemination of certain modes of thought, and certain ways of posing and resolving questions involving the entire subsequent development of national life.' (1971: 184.)

The conditions of the late 1970s certainly created a more favourable terrain for the 'mode of thought' which the New

Right represented. Their success lay in their ability to place corporate liberalism and the expanded state in the front line of explanations of crisis and questions about the 'entire development of national life'.

A LONG GESTATION:
THE RISE OF THE NEW RIGHT

There is general agreement among commentators on the American New Right that its political genesis lay in the unsuccessful campaign for the Republican Presidential nomination by Barry Goldwater in 1964. Goldwater's campaign brought together many of the themes and issues which have subsequently become the central elements of the ideology and politics of the New Right: a strident anti-communism; a hostility to state interference, particularly in the form of welfare intervention; and a conservative populism (Saloma 1984; White and Gill 1981). The years between Goldwater's failure in 1964 and Reagan's success in 1980 saw the simultaneous domination of national politics by the culture of corporate liberalism and the creation of a massive organizational infrastructure of the New Right: what John Saloma has called 'the new conservative labyrinth' (1984). This infrastructure set out to learn the lessons of the successes and failures of the Goldwater campaign, and to channel them into the reconstruction of national politics against the liberal hegemony. The first target, the precondition for a possible conservative hegemony, was the Republican party itself: the task, to break the élite 'Eastern establishment's' hold over the party machinery and ideology. Links were constructed between the representatives of old conservatism and the emergent radical right of republicanism. The creation of an institutional infrastructure was intended to facilitate a connection between the organizational struggles over political machinery and processes with the ideological struggles in the political culture against the errors of liberalism.

There are three aspects of this emergent institutional infrastructure which need to be addressed here. First is the creation of an array of conservative think-tanks – led by such organizations as the American Enterprise Institute, the Hoover Institute and the

Heritage Foundation – as the ideological/policy alternatives to what were seen as liberal establishment foundations (the Ford Foundation and the Institute for Policy Studies, for example). The new conservative institutes pulled together and publicized the intellectual armoury of the New Right, especially in the areas of economic and public policy and foreign affairs. The institutes and think-tanks have been the beneficiaries of massive funding from corporate sources. For example, Karen Rothmeyer (1981) estimated that over 12 years, 22 different New Right organizations received over $100 million from Richard Scaife and the Scaife family foundations. Other corporate foundations were equally generous in promoting the development of the new conservative infrastructure (see Saloma 1984, Chapter 3).

Secondly, the 1970s saw a massive growth in the range of New Right political organizations linking fundraising, the training of putative political candidates, the targetting of liberal politicians; organizing direct mail campaigns, the preparation of policy agendas; the assessment of voting records and a variety of other organizational tasks for the New Right. Once again, there are strong links in the development of this infrastructure between the old conservatives and the emergent radical right, both in terms of personnel and in terms of their political focal points. Although their political roots can be traced back to organizations such as William Buckley's Young Americans for Freedom, and the range of bodies which surrounded the Goldwater campaign of 1964, the mushrooming of New Right organizations began in earnest in the early 1970s, when the creation of Political Action Committees (PACs) provided a crucial link between funding sources, new political tactics (such as Richard Viguerie's development of direct mailing) and the organizational energies of the New Right. The Federal Election Commission's study in 1980 established that the three largest PACs (in terms of revenue) were all conservative organizations: led by Senator Jesse Helm's National Congressional Club and Terry Dolan's National Conservative PAC (Saloma 1984: 46).

Thirdly, the emergent New Right infrastructure facilitated the construction of links between the different fractions of the New Right: the old conservatives; the old radical right (such as the John Birch Society); the libertarian intellectuals and political activists (Friedman, Laffer, Simon); the neo-conservatives (one time liberals who recanted in order to save liberalism from itself, like Daniel Bell and Irving Kristol); the growing body of Christian Fundamentalism (the 'Moral Majority') and the corporate funders. John Saloma has summarized his detailed analysis of the infrastructure of the New Right in the following description:

> I visualize the conservative New Right as a pyramid divided into three layers. (For this image I am indebted to Gross [1980] who described three groups: leaders who provide strategic guidance, executive managers and members.) I hypothesize that efective power rests with the leaders, a group of wealthy conservatives who have funded it since its beginnings in the 1950s . . . I will designate this as the conservative finance group. A more visible second tier of leadership, the executive managers, form what I will refer to as the strategy/operations group. Familiar names in the upper echelons are candidates for membership in this hypothetical group: W. Glenn Campbell of the Hoover Institution, Irving Kristol, William E. Simon, the late William Baroody Sr. of AEI, Melvin Laird and Richard Viguerie among others. The third layer of the pyramid includes the majority of those visibly active in the network, especially the relatively young or new faces who dominate the media – Terry Dolan of NCPAC, Howard Phillips of the Conservative Caucus, the Reverend Jerry Falwell and the electronic ministers . . . the hundreds of conservative intellectuals – and form a network of subordinate communications and action groups. (1984: 139)

The existence of this organizational infrastructure made possible the pulling together of the diverse field of ideological positions that are represented within the political culture of the New Right. The New Right is not one distinct political ideology; rather it draws together themes from a variety of ideological sources, and has articulated them into a temporary political unity which involves the suppression of difference as much as it involves the creation of agreement. The following section deals with some of the ideological strands of the alliance which the New Right represents, and the conditions of the ideological and political alliance which was constructed.

AN UNHOLY ALLIANCE:
THE NEW RIGHT

There are three main tributaries which have fed the ideological development of the New Right in the USA: economic liberalism (sometimes called neo-liberalism); neo-conservatism; and moral traditionalism.[3] Each of these contributes distinctive elements of the political agenda of the New Right, but each also contains elements which represent potential ideological contradictions with the other positions. The creation of the New Right as an ideological and political alliance required ideological work to make these elements fit together, and to suppress potential points of difference and tension within the alliance.

The revitalization of economic liberalism played a central role in the construction of the New Right in two ways. Firstly, it provided the fundamental intellectual rationale for the presentation of the New Right's economic agenda: defining economic problems as the result of state interference in the free play of market forces. It linked macro-economic issues (the overall functioning of the economy) with the micro issues (personal taxation and individual enterprise) through the uniting themes of freedom and anti-statism. Wherever one touched this new liberalism, it identified the same blockages to economic development: the state through regulation or taxation or social policy exerted a deadening influence on initiative and enterprise: whether corporate or individual. The popularization of this economics made explicit its underlying social philosophies and political assumptions. An atomistic model of society as composed of free individuals was counterposed with the artificial interventions of the state. Wealth creation (and the trickle-down effect for the less wealthy) was seen as being stifled by unnecessary regulation, interference and 'legalized robbery' (taxation). These elements were condensed in a bi-polar model of politics which opposed the minimal state and the totalitarian state:

A critical principle which must be communicated forcefully to the American public is the inexorable interdependence of economic wealth and individual liberty. Our citizens must learn that what keeps them prosperous is production and technological innovation. Their wealth emerges, not from government offices or politicians' edicts, but only from that part of the market-place which is *free*. They must also be taught to understand the relationship among collectivism, centralized planning, and poverty so that every new generation of Americans need not naively receive the Marxist revelations afresh. (Simon 1979: 235.)

The sponsored development of this revival of economic liberalism through many of the New Right think-tanks was not particularly surprising. It provided the intellectual rationale for the emergent business agenda of corporate capital. It theorized the initiatives which leading sectors of US capital sought in practice: deregulation; the freedoms of accumulation; and the reduction of taxation. Its achievement was to develop an approach that linked this corporate agenda to an individualistic economics: the behaviour of the corporations was nothing more than the behaviour of individuals writ large. They had the same goals (freedom to pursue wealth and happiness); the same driving forces (initiative and enterprise); and suffered from the same *malaise* (excessive state interference). The construction of this equivalence between corporate and individual experience was central to the establishment of the business agenda as a national political task.

The second major strand of New Right ideology was provided by neo-conservatism, whose objective was the reconstruction of traditional American political values which had been betrayed by the élite, corporatist, liberalism of the 1960s and 70s (see Coser and Howe eds, 1977). Where economic liberalism highlighted the economic excesses of the state, neo-conservatism highlighted its political excesses. In the eyes of the neo-conservatives, corporate liberalism had gone too far by turning the state into an agency of social reconstruction. Seduced in the 1960s by foreign ideologies of equality, corporate liberalism had used the state to dismantle traditional values and social practices with the intent of promoting new social arrangements. James Q. Wilson presents this neo-conservative view of the liberal failure to appreciate traditional values:

Among élites, however, the interest in a communal as opposed to an individualistic public philosophy . . . often based on a desire, not to perfect character by moral development, but to repudiate the philistine features of an ordinary culture with its commonplace concerns for conventional morality and personal propriety. (1983: 238.)

What was worse was that such initiatives at social reform were doomed to failure. Writers such as Patrick Moynihan and Nathan Glazer argued that the use of state programmes to construct social reform through education, housing and welfare policies inevitably produced unintended negative consequences; undermined existing patterns of social arrangements; led to an unrealistic level of rising expectations among the would-be beneficiaries of equality; placed increasing burdens on the state; and, most significantly, threatened to shatter the central (if not eternal) place of liberal individualism at the heart of American political culture. The neo-conservative attack on corporate liberalism had two main focal points: one domestic, one international.

Neo-conservatism's domestic focus was on the expansion of the state's social programmes, particularly the Kennedy/Johnson Great Society programme and its aftermath. It was here that the state could be found intruding more and more into the realm of individual freedoms to sponsor social and economic mobility and equality for whole groups of the population. At the heart of these developments was an alliance between élite liberals, the leaders and ideologues of the new social movements, and the 'New Class' of professional social reformers, welfare workers and state employees to promote the continued expansion of the state. This concept of the New Class has played a central role in the neo-conservative attack on welfare. The state professionals – rather than welfare clients – are seen as both the main architects and the main beneficiaries of the expanded state. It is they who have vested professional and bureaucratic interests in the defence of state programmes, and their further expansion. And it was they who were responsible for the undermining of established social values and practices:

There was an operative distinction, however unspoken, between the now-traditional New Deal aspects of the welfare state, which dealt with basic economic needs, and those of the Great Society which, it was felt, were directed more to remedying inequality, particularly racial inequality. Uniting all these hostilities was anger at the bureaucrats and professionals who administered these programs. It was these liberals who led the advance towards cultural nihilism and who disdained and walked over the traditionalists of the silent majority. (Hunter 1981: 314.)

If corporate liberalism had the effect of promoting cultural nihilism domestically, its effect on the USA's international position was viewed as equally destructive. In this the neo-conservatives aligned directly with an older variety of conservatism's virulent anti-communism. Liberalism had contributed to the undermining of national moral fibre in the Vietnam era: withdrawal and humiliation being the result of a treacherous alliance of the corrosive cynicism of the mass media; élite liberal weakness and the noisy minority of students and other radicals. The result in neo-conservative eyes was a post-Vietnam and post-Watergate loss of national direction resulting from liberal equivocation which culminated in the vacillations and failures of the Carter administration. *Détente* with the Soviet Union, the betrayal of friendly anti-communist regimes (particularly in Central and South America) because of liberal obsessions with human rights, the cancelling of the B1 bomber programme, the Iran hostage crisis – all bore testimony to the catastrophic effect of élite liberalism on the USA's role on the world stage.

The final ideological strand of the New Right has some significant overlaps with neo-conservatism, not least in the focus on the decay and corrosion of traditional values by corporate liberalism. This strand is one of moral traditionalism, combining the revival of religious fundamentalism with a variety of anti-liberal single issue movements and organizations (such as anti-abortion, anti-Equal Rights Amendment, anti-gay groupings). If economic liberalism and neo-conservatism can be seen as defining the economic and political excesses of liberalism, moral authoritarianism has performed the task of defining and attacking the cultural excesses of liberalism. Corporate liberalism was accused of promoting cultural modernism and cultural nihilism at the expense of the traditional values of the moral majority (sometimes known as Moral Majority Inc., the organization founded by Jerry Falwell). The moral authoritarian strand orchestrated a range of protests on a variety of social issues, linked by what might be described as a pro-family stance: against abortion, against feminism (and the Equal Rights Amendment in particular), against homosexuality, against atheistic teaching and school books – and for traditional gender roles, family organization, parental power. In this, as Alan Crawford (1980) has argued, there has been a distinctive alliance between the male ministers and traditionalist women, such as Phyllis Schaffly and Anita Bryant. The magazine *Christian Voice* provided this definition of the moral right's agenda in its statement of purpose:

> We believe that the unmistakable signs of moral decay are all around us: sexual promiscuity, legalized abortion, the disparaging of marriage, family and the role of motherhood – all are rampant in our schools, our government, and even in many churches. The primary objective of *Christian Voice* is to slice through this murky sea of non-values and clearly focus public attention on the basic moral implications of each issue along with its ultimate political consequences. (quoted in Young 1982: 101.)

The rise of evangelical fundamentalism – the form of televangelism (or the television ministries of Falwell, Robertson, Swaggart and others) have created a significant cultural dimension to the development of the New Right, including control over means of cultural production and distribution through the televison ministries, which have linked a religious fundamentalism on social issues (Christian values) to an equally fundamentalist American nationalism through the metaphor of 'God-fearing Americans' opposed to 'godless' communists, atheists, liberals and others of that ilk. The success of the ministries in linking traditional fundamentalist morality to modern communications technologies has been substantial: in recruitment, fund-raising and the mobilization of their memberships around social and political issues (Saloma 1984; Young 1982; Conway and Siegelman 1984).

While it is convenient to use an analogy which identifies each of these three strands of the New Right as respectively contributing the economic, political and cultural agendas of the New Right, it nevertheless oversimplifies both the ways in which these different tributaries have overlapped with one another and the points at which their different responses to the 'crisis' of America involve significant tensions. The three tributaries are aligned in a view of a generalized sense of crisis of American values, for which corporate liberalism is held responsible. Whether in infringing freedoms, imposing taxation, corrupting values, being soft on communism, promoting cultural diversity or undermining the family – the liberalism of the 1960s and 70s stands at the heart of the New Right's demonology. Within this, it is possible to see how different elements of their agendas intersect. The rhetorical power of individual freedoms derives from the intersection of economic liberalism's revival of classical political economy's insistence on the free market rights of the individual to dispose of his (very rarely her) goods and abilities, with neo-conservatism's concern to reassert individualism as the centre piece of American political culture and evangelical fundamentalism's commitment to the rights and responsibilities of the individual. (Not that they have necessarily read Max Weber, but there is certainly a practical understanding of the power of the Protestant Ethic and its social and economic resonances.)

These intersections of anti-collectivist and pro-individualist sentiments in the three tributaries are condensed in an imagery of America: a profound and distinctive nationalism. This combines domestic and external elements in evoking a symbolism of a national mission. For economic liberalism, the USA has been, and could be once again, the powerhouse and exemplar of competitive individualism: the proof that free-market capitalism works (set against the demonstrable failings of planned or command economies, Soviet style). As such, the USA has a responsibility to 'put its own house in order' and present the rest of the world with a model economy. For neo-conservatism, the USA was the inheritor of the best of the European traditions of political culture, its liberal individualism, without the blockages of status and class which had inhibited European development. As such, America has a responsibility to demonstrate the full flowering of this liberal 'possessive individualism', and to resist the international political development of opposed forces: in the form of international communism. For the moral authoritarians, the moral values of a civic culture which rests on what

Paul Johnson has called the 'tripod' of the family, the church and the minimal state represent a harmonization of 'Man, Society and God': whose perfection needs strong defence against the enemies within and without (Fitzgerald 1983). These rhetorics combine in a sense of national importance and world mission, whose impetus has been undermined from within. Once more, corporate liberalism was the guilty party: inducing and exacerbating the post-Vietnam and post-Watergate national guilt to subvert American pride and American commitment to sustaining the USA's (God-given) historical task of bringing freedom to the rest of the world. (The role of the media in this process – a central feature of the New Right's attack on liberal corruption of values – is worthy of far more extensive discussion. For the moment, though, it is enough to note that it was the media which brought the war home and put Nixon on trial: two unforgivable, and unforgiven, sins.)

Beneath this surface unity of the New Right there are a variety of unresolved ideological tensions. At the heart of these are the libertarian implications of economic liberalism: the social and cultural consequences of the commitment to economic freedom. One distinctive impact of the revival of economic liberalism in Western capitalism has been the way in which these libertarian implications have been taken up, both ideologically by those committed to a variety of deregulations not necessarily on the initial prospectus of the academic progenitors of economic liberalism (for example, the de-criminalization of drugs and prostitution), and practically by those groups who are able to invest high earnings and tax cuts in the lifestyles of the consumer culture.

Maddox and Lillie (1984) have argued that there exists a distinct political identity of libertarians: a small but significant (and growing) grouping who, in the past, have not been addressed either by the traditional Republican conservatism (economically liberal but socially conservative) nor by traditional Democratic liberalism (because of the statist quality in its mixture of social liberalism and economic conservatism). This libertarian potential – the possibility of a thorough going social and cultural individualism alongside economic individualism – sits uncomfortably beside the moral and social conservatism of both the neo-conservatives and (most dramatically) the moral authoritarians. Given their commitments to the restoration of traditional values in political and cultural terms, neither strand could tolerate a radically libertarian culture of individualism. The tension is dramatically exposed in Milton and Rose Friedman's *The Tyranny of the Status Quo* (1984). In Chapter 6, devoted to 'Unemployment, the smokestack industries, tariffs', they are concerned to demonstrate that 'deregulation' continues to be an economic imperative. The chapter ends with a paeon of praise to the entrepreneurial spirit which enables people to be economically active in an over-regulated economy:

> As we have found to be true again and again, *the best ground for hope is the ingenuity and fertility of the market in getting around governmental restrictions.* We have an expanding underground economy that is no respecter of governmentally imposed restrictions. The small entrepreneurs who set up their stands along Fisherman's Wharf in San Francisco, on Fifth Avenue and other thoroughfares in New York, and wherever there are customers to be found demonstrate the strength of market forces, the widespread impulse of people to be independent, to do their own thing. (1984: 130; emphasis in the original.)

Aside from remarking on the fact that the Friedmans' move from Chicago to the West Coast has added a peculiarly anachronistic counter-cultural rhetoric to their economic liberalism, this passage is intriguing for the way in which economic liberalism legitimates law-breaking. The following chapter discusses a variety of social processes which contribute to crime. This includes some classic positions of economic liberalism (the expansion of the state undermining a culture of individual responsibility) and of libertarianism (the multiplication of the number of laws causes a rise in crime). However, the Friedmans also offer this view:

> A closely associated development has been the change in the character of the family. Statistics on divorce, one-parent families, and illegitimate births demonstrate that the nuclear family is losing its traditional role. The family no longer serves as an integrative institution, as a vehicle for instilling values and developing standards of behavior. Nothing has taken its place. As a result, an increasing number of our youth grow

up without any firm values, with little understanding of 'right'
and 'wrong', with few convictions that will discipline their
appetites. (1984: 135.)

Now it is clearly possible to derive a variety of textual pleasures from this happy juxtaposition of chapters and arguments.
'Illegitimate births' could be viewed as yet another tribute to
the 'widespread impulse of people to be independent' and to
elude unnecessary governmental regulation. One might reverse
the propositions and argue that corporate crime, tax fraud, the
'Contragate' scandal, and so forth, are the consequence of the
decline of the American family (Oliver North as the sad victim
of a broken home?). Such jollity (and heartfelt appreciation
for their confession that 'We are not criminologists', p. 133)
aside, what is striking here is the interruption of a text of
economic liberalism by arguments whose natural home is that
of neo-conservatism and moral authoritarianism: the family
instilling values, disciplining appetites and its contemporary
breakdown (see, for example, James Q. Wilson 1983).

Formally, then, the libertarianism of economic liberalism
stands in tension with the reconstruction of traditional values
sought in the rhetoric of both the neo-conservatives and moral
authoritarians. It is difficult to imagine the evangelists or the
neo-conservative ideologues going along with the Friedmans'
conclusion that illicit drugs ought to be de-criminalized, for
example. The promotion of individual choice – consumer choice
– involves precisely the creation of that form of cultural nihilism
which is abhorred by the other elements of the New Right. The
market-place is not in the business of moral evaluation, merely
that of setting a price.

This interruption of the family into the otherwise rigourous
individualism of the Friedmans' arguments should alert us to one
of the crucial points at which the different New Right tributaries
flow together. Behind the individualism of the economic liberals
stands an implicit view of the family, rather than the individual,
as the basic unit of society (Fitzgerald 1983). It is the family
which earns (through its male breadwinner) chooses and con-
sumes (through its female domestic labourer), and passes on
the values of individualism. This elision of the individual and
the family (and of economic liberalism and neo-conservatism) is

most visible in the writings of George Gilder, leavened with a little socio-biological reasoning about the causes and consequences of sexual difference (for example, Gilder 1981). Although the placing of the family is different in each of the three different constituent elements of the New Right, it plays a key role in the creation of an apparent ideological unity of the New Right.[4]

Before examining this in more detail in the following section, it is also worth noting some of the elisions in the rhetorical vocabulary of the New Right which facilitate the appearance of unity. Central among these are the equivalences which are struck between what might appear to be different interests addressed by the New Right. The ideological field of the New Right identifies a symmetry of the individual, the family, the corporation and the nation in relation to the impulses of freedom, deregulation, and national pride. Each is fostered and strengthened by the same set of political commitments. The maintenance of this tenuous symmetry and the sustaining of the apparent unity of the different tributaries of the New Right has required both organizational and ideological work: the public management of potentially conflicting discourses, in which the role played by Ronald Reagan has been central.

The place of Reagan in the construction of the American New Right is a difficult one to disentangle from the variety of forms in which he has been mythologized: autocue reader; the 'Teflon' President; Reagan the Contra; Reagan asleep; Reagan the voice of freedom; the 'fact-free' President and on and on. In some ways, this array of imagery may itself be a clue to the role played by Reagan: the actor president whose performances lend themselves as much to a sceptical or oppositional iconography as they do to their intended iconic effects: the strong leader who's just an everyday guy; the president who can 'mis-speak the truth' with complete sincerity. In assessing Reagan, this element of performance is an essential dimension (what Larry Grossberg (1988) has called the Reagan 'affect'). While the level of Reagan's popularity as a President may have been overstated (Ferguson and Rogers 1986), the 'performance' includes a supra-political quality of Reagan 'as man', 'as leader' and as embodiment of American values.[5] In relation to the New Right, this quality of performance is significant in terms of a ventriloqual capacity to draw on the different rhetorical contributions of the three strands of New Right ideology, without the seams showing. Reagan has provided a seemingly effortless ability to shift between the imagery and metaphors of economic liberalism, neo-conservatism and moral traditionalism – speaking their unity.

THE REAL THREAT:
TARGETTING WELFARE

The Soviet Union is the immediate danger perceived by Americans. Yet it is not the real threat to our national security. The real threat is the welfare state . . . (Friedman and Friedman 1984: 73.)

Although the precise choice between the welfare state and the Soviet Union (or, as it is more often referred to, World Communism) for the role of greatest danger to the USA's national security remains something of a moot point within the New Right, there is no doubt that the Friedmans' election of welfare to this high office accurately captures important sentiments of the New Right. Welfare has come to occupy this highly visible position because it condenses a wide variety of central themes in New Right ideology, deriving from neo-liberalism, neo-conservatism and moral traditionalism.

It is best to begin from the terrain of public spending, since this provided an initial political springboard for the New Right both in the USA and Britain. The growth of public spending in the 1960s and 70s was identified by the economic liberals and politicians of the New Right as the major cause of recession and stagflation. Reagan, like the Conservatives under Thatcher, initially campaigned for the need to reduce public spending rather than to abolish public welfare systems, and linked the need to control public spending to an attack on 'waste, abuse and fraud'. One distinctive feature of New Right rhetoric has been to draw definite limits around what was meant by public spending, restricting its usage to spending by the state on social programmes. Joel Krieger (1987) has argued that the New Right created a new way of resolving the contradiction, identified by such authors as James O'Connor

(1973), between the legitimation and accumulation functions of the capitalist state, by moving the terrain of legitimation. The agenda for legitimation was reshaped around the 'fiscal crisis of the state' via 'the manipulation of fiscal policy and economic rationale to make working class and underclass demands appear incompatible with rational economic goals and the "national interest"' (Krieger 1987: 179). The consequence was that 'deficit politics became the ideological basis for the two themes of Reaganism: imperial defence and fiscal rectitude' (Krieger 1987: 180). The starting point for the New Right attack on welfare became the issue of what 'we' could afford. Indeed, as both defence spending and the deficit rose in the Reagan years, the fiscal crisis squeeze on public spending on social programmes intensified.

For the economic liberals and the Reaganauts, the excess of public spending manifested itself not only in its inflationary consequences, but also in its effects on enterprise through taxation. The growing tax burden at both national and local levels was seen as being responsible for business decline and capital flight in search of more favourable environments, that is, those with lower taxes alongside other desirable attributes. The enterprise of both individuals and corporations was seen as being stifled by high rates of taxation – and the successes of local 'taxpayers' revolts' (such as California's Proposition 13) signalled a linkage between the 'business agenda' of corporate capital and popular anxiety about taxation levels (Adams 1984). Although, as Cronin and Radtke (1987) argue, the rise in personal taxation in the 1970s was partly the effect of personal taxes substituting for the declining share of the national tax bill being paid from corporate taxes (combined with the effects of inflation), this shift between corporate and personal tax burdens was largely invisible. Cronin and Radtke identify the link which the New Right were able to make between taxation and social programme spending:

> With the tax shift away from large corporations and affluent individuals largely hidden, enough voters were ready to believe Political Action Committees representing the business community, who said that tax increases were caused by burgeoning expenditures for a federal government 'out of control'. Programmes recently created during the 'Great

Society' could be isolated and their recipients stigmatised as the culprits. (1987: 280.)

The stigmatization of the 'Great Society' welfare programmes, dating from the Kennedy and Johnson administrations, involves a number of dimensions in which economic liberalism and neo-conservatism find considerable common ground. The connections can be found by exploring what the Friedmans have called 'The Iron Triangle' – the collection of interests which sustain the status quo in the face of attempts to change it: 'At one corner are the direct beneficiaries of a law; at a second, the legislative committees and their staffs; at a third, the bureaucracy administering a law.' (1984: 42.) The middle of these three corners is not particularly a concern here, not least because of the way the new realism resulting from Reagan's successes, politically and organizationally, exerted a substantial grip on the hearts and minds of other elected representatives after 1981. We shall come to the direct beneficiaries shortly, but it is best to begin with the 'bureaucrats', for this category provides one of the tightest intersections between the economic liberals and the neo-conservatives. For the economic liberals, the problem of a bureaucratized system of welfare provision is its lack of accountability (where accountability is to be understood in terms of a profit and loss account). Bureaucrats lack the discipline of market forces, and their inherent tendency is towards bureaucratic imperialism: the enlargement of their budget or numbers of staff on the payroll. They have an occupational commitment to sustaining or enlarging the programme which employs them:

Bureaucracies themselves should be assumed to be noxious, authoritarian parasites on society, with a tendency to augment their own size and power and to cultivate a parasitical clientele in all classes of society ... People must be taught to start calling for a rollback of the bureaucracy, where nothing will be lost but strangling regulation and where the gains will always take the form of liberty, productivity and jobs. (Simon 1979: 235.)

This 'lack of discipline' would be bad enough in itself, but for the neo-conservatives, the bureaucrats and workers employed by the state's social programmes have acquired the characteristics of a social class: the 'New Class'. The New Class refers to the massive increase in professional and white collar workers employed by the state since the 1960s, many in the expanded welfare, anti-poverty and other programmes of the Great Society. For the neo-conservatives, this expansion resembles a distinctive class grouping, with its own definite economic position (state salaries), its own corresponding ideology (collectivist or quasi-socialist, seeing the state as an agency of reform and progress) and a corresponding politics (the further promotion of the corporate liberal vision of social improvement).[6]

The neo-conservative hostility to this New Class is intense, since it represents both the progenitor and product of those tendencies which the neo-conservatives identify as having undermined traditional American values. Elements of the New Class's social outlook are supposed to include an excessive enthusiasm for equality; a 'blaming the system' ideology; the promotion of cultural modernism/nihilism, including a commitment to rationalist planning; an exaltation of the public realm (the state) at the expense of the private (the family); and, as with all such varieties of liberalism, being the thin end of the 'red wedge', or the start of the slippery slope to socialism. This view of the New Class is shared, though more virulently, by the moral traditionalists who identify the progressivism of the New Class as the driving force behind the corruption of conventional morality and culture:

> It is no wonder that we find America depraved, decadent and demoralised today…The godless minority of treacherous individuals who have been permitted to formulate national policy must now realize that they do not represent the majority. They must be made to see that moral Americans are a powerful group who will no longer permit them to destroy our country with their godless, liberal principles. (Falwell, introduction to R. Viguerie *The New Right: We're Ready*, quoted in Young 1982: 62.)

This New Class, and the liberal ideology which it embodies, are accused of using the state to engage in social engineering – the promotion of rights and equalities – which undercut the independence of individuals and interfere (unnecessarily) in the private realms of both the market and the family. Social engineering is visible in a variety of areas: equal rights in relation to race, gender and sexuality; abortion; school integration ('bussing'); and the general elevation of professional ideology over private wisdom (which usually means parental wisdom). Schooling, both because of bussing and the issue of parental control, has been one of the front lines of the New Right attack:

> According to the Bible, God has charged parents, not civil governments, with responsibility for the rearing of children. All education is rooted in values. The question is whose values shall prevail? Those of the parent, or those of the state? In a free society, the family, rather than the state, ought to determine whether children shall be subjected to pornography, amorally premised sex education, atheistically based textbooks and curriculum, or proselytization for doctrines of homosexuality, abortion and extra-marital sex. (Howard Phillips, statement to White House Conference on Families, quoted in Young, 1982: 115.)

Such social engineering undermines existing cultures or value systems (for example, the forced integration of school bussing means that children are taken away from the culture of the community in which their parents have chosen to live). In place of stable value systems, the professional wisdom of the social engineers promotes a condition of normlessness: a state of cultural nihilism. In addition to undermining the culture of the family, this same ideology has wrought changes in the structure of the family, promoting women's employment and illegitimacy (through welfare payments to single parent families in the Aid to Families with Dependent Children – AFDC – programme).

Finally, the welfare system stands accused of promoting 'demoralization': breaking the structure of work incentives which, for both economic liberals and neo-conservatives, are an essential feature of the workings of a successful economic system. Although economic liberalism's and neo-conservatism's views of human nature are rather different (the former stressing the spirit of enterprise, the latter the principle of discomfort avoidance), both are united in their commitment to a system of welfare support which maintains the incentive to work, rather than providing an alternative to the wage. The 'Great Society' welfare programmes are seen as having promoted dis-employment, creating a dependent poor and a demoralized, independence sapping, culture of poverty.

BEING POOR, BEING BLACK: THE POLITICS OF RACE AND WELFARE

Many of these arguments come together in Charles Murray's *Losing Ground* (1984), a neo-conservative *tour de force* on the errors and effects of the expansion of public welfare in the 1960s and 70s. Murray provides a sustained critique of the poverty programmes with the aim of demonstrating the way in which they have 'demoralized' the poor because of the incorrect (élite liberal) assumptions on which they were premissed. However, one the most striking features of the book is the way in which Murray gives a central role to one of the implicit presumptions of the New Right politics of welfare: that welfare is about race. Murray uses statistical rates and comparisons for black Americans as indicators of the effects of the welfare programmes on the poor. This is self-consciously justified on the basis of the absence of longitudinal data about the poor in general, and that data referring to black Americans serves as the best available proxy for disadvantaged or poor: 'The comparison between black (or "black and others") and white is an imprecise but nonetheless useful comparison over time between "disadvantaged" Americans in general (blacks) and "advantaged" Americans in general (whites), blurred by the members of both groups who fail to fit their category.' (1984: 55.) This, as Murray recognizes, is a less than satisfactory index of disadvantage (there being over twice as many white Americans as black living below the poverty line), but it does focus the story nicely. Absent from the text, however, is any attempt to compare the data for black Americans which Murray uses to illustrate the effects of the poverty programme with any evidence for 'poor whites' (that is, evidence which would distinguish the effects of poverty and/or poverty programmes from the effects of race). This allows Murray to elide the categories of poor and black to considerable effect, such that consequences attributed to the poverty programmes come to sit quite naturally alongside arguments about the black experience and black culture. The narrative effect of this statistical device is to 'ghettoize' poverty and its attendant demoralization within black America.

Murray's main concern is to demonstrate the effect of poverty programmes on key indices of black social behaviour: labour force participation (down dramatically for young black males); illegitimate births (dramatically up for young black females); the number of single-parent families (dramatically up among blacks); and the number of homicide victims (disproportionately up among blacks). The core of Murray's argument starts out from an economic rationalism: that people assess the consequences of their choices on a straightforward economic calculus, summarized by Murray in his Premise 1: 'People respond to incentives and disincentives. Sticks and carrots work.' (1984: 146).[7]

From this starting point, Murray is able to argue that the poverty programmes changed the 'rules of the game', shifting the calculus, so that the poor were invited to make behavioural choices which had short-term rationality, but were destructively demoralizing in the long term. Thus a short-term rational choice to become dependent on welfare led to the loss of those behaviours and attitudes (job search and two-parent families) which provided routes out of poverty. If this were the sole line of argument of the book, it would be a straightforward text of economic liberalism; but these arguments about calculations are only a subtext of the main argument: the destruction of an anti-poverty culture in America by the poverty programmes and the ideology which informed them. In Chapter 14, Murray deals with the 'destruction of status rewards' in which he argues that the 'Great Society' reforms destroyed a cultural system of status which had previously promoted escape from poverty (the 'American way' of social mobility) by removing the moral distinction between the deserving and undeserving poor. He presents two propositions: (1) Status was withdrawn from the low-income, independent working family, with disastrous consequences to the quality of life for such families; (2) Status was withdrawn from the behaviors that engendered escape from poverty. (1984: 179.)

In effect, the 'Great Society' programmes 'homogenized' the poor, abolishing the status distinctions within them, especially that concerned with pride in independence and self-sufficiency:

> The unwillingness to acknowledge moral inequality was a hallmark of the Great Society social programs and persisted throughout the 1970s. It was not just that the squeaky hinges (the failures) got the oil. Administrators of programs made Kafkaesque rules to avoid revealing that some poor people are brighter or of better character or more industrious than others. (1984: 183.)

This cultural destruction was the effect of two imperatives which were embedded in the 'Great Society' programmes. One was to remove the stigma which was attached to welfare: without stigma, the status pressure to gain 'independence' was undermined. The second was the move (central to the liberal ideology) from a presumption that poverty was primarily a result of individual circumstances and character to poverty seen as a result of the failure of the system. Such a view of poverty, whether objectively true or not, undermines the psychological investment which people must make in social mobility. It runs counter to the central mythology of America culture.

The promotion of this systemic view of poverty was the result of a tangled intersection of white élite liberalism and the civil rights movement in the 1960s. Policy makers succumbed to a systemic view of poverty (propagated by social scientists), partly motivated by white liberal guilt about the condition of Black America. The outcome has been to reinforce the tendencies within ghetto culture towards a lack of faith in the system, and to remove incentives towards individual social mobility.

It is worth remarking that racism appears as a factor in the condition of black Americans on a surprisingly small number of occasions, given the book is about this condition. It is not that racism is a concept of which Murray disapproves, or wishes to avoid. Indeed, it makes a fleeting appearance as a process which creates 'devastating effects . . . on self-confidence' (p. 187), but only to describe a condition which has been exacerbated by post-1964 social policy. In the chapter on employment, for example, it never gets a mention. For the most part, social policy and its black 'victims' appear to exist in a social and economic vacuum.

The systemic view of poverty provides 'official sanction to reject personal responsibility for one's actions' (1984: 189), which breaches one of the central tenets of both economic liberalism and neo-conservatism, expressed by Murray as his 'Premiss 3: People must be held responsible for their actions. Whether they *are* responsible or not in some ultimate philosophical or biochemical sense cannot be the issue if society is to function' (1984: 146, emphasis in original). This brings us to the core of Murray's argument: that the liberal intelligentsia of the 1960s promoted a social policy which was misconceived, had unintended consequences, attributed blame to the system and – its most glaring error – was at odds with 'popular wisdom'. This popular wisdom plays a crucial role in Murray's narrative. It is the historical Subject which was ignored by the liberals in the 1960s, when:

> for the blue-collar and white-collar electorate, not much changed. For them, the welfare cheats and loafers still loomed large, and sturdy self-reliance was still a chief virtue. For them, criminals ought to be locked up, students ought to shut up and do what the teacher says, demonstrators ought to go home and stop interrupting traffic. (1984: 42)

This is the Subject which has returned to haunt the liberals in the 1980s, when at last a new intelligentsia (no need to guess which one) has brought about a new 'synthesis of wisdoms', aligning élite wisdom with popular wisdom: 'the views to be heard in most discussions in most blue-collar bars or country club lounges in most parts of the United States. It is the inarticulate constellation of worries and suspicions that helped account for Ronald Reagan's victory in 1980' (1984: 146). This is the classic populist interpellation of the contemporary New Right: the construction of a (implicitly majoritarian) popular opinion whose views are embodied in the agenda of the New Right itself against the socially and politically isolated élite liberals. What, then, are the elements of this popular wisdom?

The popular wisdom is characterized by hostility towards welfare (it makes people lazy), toward lenient judges (they encourage crime), and toward socially conscious schools (too busy busing kids to teach them how to read). The popular wisdom disapproves of favoritism toward blacks and of too many written in rights for minorities of all sorts. It says that the government is meddling far too much in things that are none of its business. (1984: 146.)

Fortunately, when stripped judiciously of its hostility and mean spirited (and often racist) invective, this popular wisdom turns out to bear a remarkable similarity to the wisdom of the neo-conservative intelligentsia . . .[8]

HEARTS, MINDS AND WALLETS: THE QUESTION OF HEGEMONY

The rise of the New Right in Britain and the USA has contributed to an increase of interest in the political and theoretical analyses of Antonio Gramsci, concerning the state, ideology, politics, 'common-sense' and the question of hegemony. In part, this reflects Gramsci's own concerns with the problems of analysing 'concrete situations' or 'conjunctures'. But it is also a consequence of the New Right's own self-consciousness about ideological work. In its populism and its self-proclaimed relationship to common sense and popular wisdom, the New Right appears to practise many of Gramsci's injunctions about the construction of hegemony.[9]

Certainly, the New Right bears all the signs of being part of a hegemonic project: the creation of popular consent for a new national direction, aiming to unblock the multiple elements of crisis in American economic, social and political formations to facilitate a new social direction. Nevertheless, one of the difficulties about analysing such a project is to estimate the strength of its success: the extent to which it has succeeded in its self-appointed task of resolving the balance of social forces into a newly stabilized alliance in support of this new national task. One of the difficulties is that the New Right represents a distinctive type of hegemonic project within Western societies, at least in the postwar period, in that it is a self-consciously intellectual and populist project, and as such it offers a peculiar temptation to intellectuals of the left to be hypnotised by its self-proclaimed unity of theory and common sense. One aim of this section, then, is to examine both the achievements of the New Right in constructing a new hegemony and its limitations.

It is clear that between 1980 and 1988, the New Right was able to construct the political conditions favourable to the restructuring of American capital along very distinctive lines. The business agenda, central to both the ideology and the political organization of the New Right, demanded a deregulatory and lower tax state to create the conditions for capital reformation. This, together with massive transfers to corporate capital through increased defence spending, has been achieved. It has fed the growing volatility of US capital, promoting its faster internationalization, its domestic geographical restructuring (the decline of the old core manufacturing sectors of the north east alongside the rise of the south/west sunbelt), its sectoral reorganization (the enormously rapid growth of the tertiary or service sector), and the unstable expansion of the financial and speculative sectors, especially in such forms as 'merger mania' and 'paper entrepreneurship' (Reich 1984; Davis 1986). In the process, it has speeded up the pace of class recomposition too. The Reagan era facilitated the attack by capital on organized labour: deunionization; concessionary wage bargaining, and the deconstruction of the corporatist agreements for major employers, although, with the exemplary exception of the Air Traffic Controllers, the state's role has been permissive rather than directive (Moody 1987). The process of class segmentation has also been speeded along: the continued (and subsidised) expansion of the technical, professional and managerial strata; the uneven decline of blue-collar manufacturing work; and the massive growth of low paid, part-time, non-unionised work in the service sector. (Bluestone and Harrison 1982; Davis 1986.)

The working out of these processes is not without its contradiction, most visible in the recurrent arguments around protectionism addressing blue-collar anxieties about the decline of traditional manufacturing (and the import-led consumer boom) together with those relatively immobile sectors of capital who have been unable to take advantage of the new internationalization. But these have remained subordinate voices in the face of the new realism of deregulation and favourable business climates. The anti-welfare policies of the Reagan administrations have intersected with this class recomposition in a number of ways. The budget reductions they have delivered have systematically fed the tax subsidization of both business and the salaried classes, supporting what Davis (1986) has described as their overconsumptionist habits. Simultaneously, the welfare reductions have made both the working and non-working poor more vulnerable to the impact of market forces in the labour market, freeing their initiative and drive to fill the expanding number of places in the predominantly black and female service sector.

This sketch of class recomposition also gives a clue to the pattern of the New Right 'hegemonic bloc': the set of class alliances which have been assembled around Reaganite republicanism. Leading sectors of US capital (especially the most volatile fractions of the sunbelt); the subsidized dominance of the defence industry in the restructuring of the manufacturing sector; the expanded middle classes (the core of the taxpayer/anti 'Great Society' revolt) and some, relatively protected, sections of the working class. This, Davis argues, is the core of the Reaganite plurality. It also represents the profound structuring of the hegemonic bloc around race. It is an alignment of primarily white classes and fractions against black: a division eerily reproduced in voting patterns in 1980, 1984 and 1988. Powerful though it is, this reading of the hegemonic bloc is predominantly an economic one – Reaganism as a portfolio of economic interests – and as such underestimates both the strength and weakness of the New Right hegemony. There are two areas in particular which need further exploration. One is the imperialist/nationalist dimension of neo-conservatism in the New Right, the other is the place of moral authoritarianism.

Both of these have deepened the hegemonic impact of the New Right. One potential caricature of Reagan is as the 'Dr Feelgood' of the USA: a neo-liberal promotion of domestic economic freedom and choice coupled with a neo-conservative invocation of the mission and strength of the USA internationally. Guilt-free consumption allied to guilt-free international power (the attempt to dissolve the 'Vietnam syndrome'). The resurgence of nationalism, with Reagan as the patriarch of the free world, played a significant part in the electoral mobilization of popular support for the New Right's political representatives. Again, this imperial nationalism condenses a substantial racial bifurcation – not entirely surprisingly given the composition of the imagery of the nation and its attributes on which this nationalism rests (a nation of pioneers rather than super-exploiting slave owners). Nevertheless, the potential militarization of US imperialism which is embedded in this neo-conservative version of nationalism has encountered some restraining limits. The pressure to intervene militarily in Central America has encountered the residues of the Vietnam syndrome alongside the spectacle of Iran/Contra-gate. Rhetorical confontations with the 'Evil Empire' have had to coexist with considerations of geo-political strategy, the rise of Gorbachev and the dissolution of the Eastern bloc. Massive popular support for coups such as the bombing of Tripoli and the 'rescue' of Grenada are found alongside profound suspicions of getting US troops ('our boys') drawn into warfare, particularly after the death of US marines in Beirut.

I argued earlier that one of the successes of Reagan was his ability to ventriloquize the different strands which combined the contradictory unity of the New Right. Nowhere has this been more visible than in relation to the themes of moral authoritarianism. Time after time, Dr Feelgood put his faith in God, the family, and traditional American values, and has benefitted from the support of white fundamentalism (yet another racial alignment in the hegemonic bloc). In spite of the contradictions between economic neo-liberalism and the social and moral conservatism of this fraction of the New Right, the alliance held together around Reagan. In terms of the composition of the hegemonic bloc, this alliance has considerable significance, adding the traditional middle classes to the new or cosmopolitan middle classes, together with substantial sectors of blue-collar and poor white people. Electorally, it has been of considerable significance, given the combination of the 'socially conservative' and fundamentalists that are interpellated through the metaphorical richness of (white) traditionalism.[10] Not the least part of that significance is that 'born again Christians' form the social group in the USA with the highest propensity to vote.

This more expansive conception of the New Right's hegemonic bloc suggests that while Davis is correct in identifying neo-liberalism as the core element, a substantial part of

the success has been Reaganism's ability to perform the ideological work which cements this neo-liberal core to a neo-
conservative nationalism and an authoritarian moral conservatism. But, alongside the more expanded conception of the bloc
which this provides, it also highlights points of potential fragility
and tension within its alliances. I shall return to this issue later,
but first it is important to explore some other aspects of the
hegemonic project of the New Right in terms of the political
culture of the USA. One of the conditions for over-reading the
hegemonic success of the New Right is a dependence on taking
soundings from the visible and institutionalized expressions of
the nation's political culture. The long gestation of the New
Right involved the assembling of the intellectual and organizational infrastructure (from research institutes to direct mailing
lists) which would permit it to move the assumptions of the
political culture away from the 'Great Society' liberals. Howard
Phillips, founder of the Conservative Caucus, described the task
to the annual convention of Young Americans for Freedom in
1979: 'Our country is going down the drain . . . we may have a
majority but we lack power . . . What is power? It is the ability
to tell others what the issues are, what the issues mean, and who
the good guys and the bad guys are. That is power.' (quoted in
Young, 1982: 115.)

At this level alone, the New Right has been formidably successful, creating an infrastructure of neo-liberal, neo-conservative
and moral majoritarian intellectuals and ideologues for every
issue which the New Right has wished to put on the agenda,
and developing new channels of communication to the public
outside the traditional structures of the party machines. They
have been able to swamp the public discourse of politics, as well
as advise and provide backup staff for New Right politicians
in private.[11] Alongside this 'agenda setting' capacity needs to
be set Reagan's personal hegemony over the mainstream mass
media. Caught between their own affirmation of the President's popularity and a fear of public mistrust and cynicism
about investigative journalism and abuses of the freedom of
the press, the media capitulated in the rightward shift of the
political centre. Alongside this, the crisis in liberalism itself
(and the rightward shift of many Democratic politicians to
neo-conservatism and neo-liberalism) produced an evacuation

of the political centre. Nobody wanted to be found standing in what they'd been told was a discredited space. In these ways, the hegemonization of the political culture by the New Right was a self-amplifying process.

As Davis has argued (1986: Chapter 7), a major process contributing to the New Right's hegemonization of the political culture has been the fracturing of liberalism in the guise of Democratic politics. Like the equivalent crisis of social democratic politics in Britain, this fragmentation of liberalism has been brought about by both the impact of the New Right (and its perceived impact), and by the internal contradictions of democratic liberalism. Containing as it did, an uneasy alliance of conservative (primarily Southern) democrats, the traditional 'New Deal' liberals and the expansionist 'Great Society' liberals, the Democratic Party was ripe for being thrown into a crisis of direction by the rise of the New Right. Increasingly, many of its leading representatives were drawn into the ground established by the New Right agenda: in the guises of social conservatism and neo-liberalism (as well as flurries of economic protectionism and fiscal conservatism). At the same time, the Party drew into itself the post-'Great Society' new politics, the extensions of US liberalism into civil rights, feminism, and other new politics, which brought both potential new constituencies and precisely the political tendencies feared by the traditional core of the Democratic Party. Such a convergence of political forces exacerbated the tensions between the social conservatism of the traditional Democratic core and the political claims of the new politics of race, gender and sexuality. The emergence of neo-liberalism as an ideology for recentring Democratic politics involved the abandonment of both the residual labourism of the Democrats (in favour of targetting the new middle classes) and the claims of the new political groupings (special interests). As Davis has documented, these tensions came to a head over the 1984 nomination campaign of Jesse Jackson and the 'Rainbow Coalition' and its threat to the white hegemony within democratic politics, and reappeared as the central axis of the Democratic nomination process in 1988.

The significant feature of this crisis of liberalism for the New Right's hegemony is the way the New Right both fostered and benefitted from the ensuing political *demobilization* which it involved. The crisis dislocated both old and new political constituencies from both effective representation and the construction of alternatives to the New Right. Its significance lies in the New Right's ability to mobilize a 'plurality' of voters (rather than a majority) in the face of a disorganized opposition. A number of commentators on the Reagan presidencies have highlighted one of the peculiar effects of this double movement of mobilization/demobilization: the lack of popular support for many of the policy directions of the Reagan administrations (for example, Salamon and Abramson 1984 and Ferguson and Rogers 1986). Ferguson and Rogers argue that surveys of public opinion in the USA have registered liberal, rather than New Right, majorities on almost every domestic social issue, as well as in the perhaps more surprising areas of foreign policy and military/nuclear spending.

Such evidence suggests that the hegemonic project of the New Right may be more tenuous than it at first appears. Ferguson and Rogers argue that the electoral pluralities behind the two Reagan victories appear to derive most of their impetus from expectations about the performance of the economy (and its consequences for personal well-being) rather than from any profound mobilization towards conservative 'conviction politics' (1986: 49–50). The success of the New Right in hegemonizing the political culture, then, has to be set against what can best be described, in Gramscian terms, as a state of 'passive consent' among the political support for the New Right: a limited and conditional acceptance rather than an active mobilization. In this light, however, the success in hegemonizing the political culture, and its demobilizing effects on forms of potential opposition, takes on even greater salience. Alongside the condition of passive consent exists a more widespread condition of passive dissent: an unmobilized (or little mobilized) array of political forces and groupings at odds with the main directions of the New Right's project. The crisis of American liberalism – and its party form, the Democrats – has ensured that such dissent has remained passive, as well as fragmented. Thus far, only the politics of the Rainbow Coalition has been addressed to mobilizing the different elements of dissent into an active political alliance, and once again (in 1988) the racial fracture that lies at the heart of the Democratic Party stifled the prospects for such a mobilization. The question of active mobilization is central to this issue, given the low levels of voter registration and voter participation in all areas of US politics. The 1984 Presidential election involved the active participation of only 55 per cent of potentially eligible voters. The 'Reagan landslide' recruited 32.3 per cent of potential voters. The uneven distribution of voter registration and participation – declining with income levels and overdetermined by race – adds even more salience to the issue of mobilization (see Ferguson and Rogers 1986 and Marable 1987).[12]

The conditions of the New Right's hegemony – and the depth of its penetration – will potentially be tested during the Bush Presidency. There is no natural successor to Reagan's ability to ventriloquize the different constituent vocabularies of the New Right and to symbolically hold together the elements which were welded together in an alliance at the end of the 1970s. The possibilities for fractures in that alliance are substantial, as I have argued earlier. The neo-liberal bloc at the core of the New Right project will sit uneasily alongside the neo-conservative and moral authoritarian constituencies. These centrifugal forces were visible in the 1988 Republican presidential primaries, as the different fractions of the New Right were represented in different candidacies, ending in the elision of old and new republicanism in the persona of George Bush. Equally uncertain are the prospects for the liberalism of the Democratic party, fragmented between competing strategies for economic management, neo-liberalism, social conservatism and the new politics of the Rainbow.

The New Right has attempted to force through a new settlement, hastening the crisis of corporate liberalism, by rearranging the social, economic and political forces of the US social formation. The neo-liberal social and economic policies which it put into place have significantly speeded up the recomposition of US capitalism, changed the political balance of forces (towards the new middle classes) and produced greater volatility and instability in the world economic-political system. At the same time, the 'fiscal crisis of the State' (the growing budget deficit) is returning to haunt the Bush administration, limiting the space for economic concessions within the alliance. Whether the potential hegemonic bloc of the New Right can survive its own internal contradictions is another matter. The mixture of neo-liberalism, neo-conservatism and moral traditionalism is, as I have argued, a potentially explosive one, particularly given the virulence with which some of the most regressive traces of anti-communist, anti-liberal, nationalist, patriarchal, homophobic and white supremacist formations of American ideology were drawn on in the construction of freedom. The unleashing of libertarian and ultra-conservative tendencies simultaneously might have been a major accomplishment of the New Right, helping to advance the process by which 'the great masses become detached from their traditional ideologies' (Gramsci, 1971: 276). But it is far from certain that the New Right has accomplished – or can accomplish – the necessary next stage of that process: a decisive realignment of the political forces which they helped to set free.

NOTES

This chapter emerged from a number of seminars which I gave in San Francisco, Chicago, Madison and Vancouver on the New Right and Welfare. It has been considerably improved by discussions with and comments from Larry Grossberg, Allen Hunter, and Leslie Roman.

1 The problem was stated by Gramsci with characteristic forcefulness:

> A common error in historico-political analysis consists in an inability to find the correct relation between what is organic and what is conjunctural. This leads to presenting causes as immediately operative which in fact only operate indirectly, or to asserting that the immediate causes are the only effective ones. In the first case there is an excess of 'economism', or doctrinaire pedantry; in the second, an excess of 'ideologism'. In the first case, there is an overestimation of mechanical causes, in the second an exaggeration of the voluntarist and individual element. (1971: 178.)

However, defining the problem is not quite the same as solving it.

2 See, for example, Hall (1988, 1989); Piven and Cloward (1982); Clarke (1982), and Clarke, Cochrane and Smart (1987).

3 The process of political recomposition has provoked a wide range of analyses of voter volatility, party realignment and political

ideology. Perhaps the most interesting is Maddox and Lillie's analysis of the 'political spectrum', which attempts to distinguish liberals, conservatives, libertarians and populists (1984). The revival of older political ideologies in new forms is reflected in both the title and approach of Medcalf and Dolbeare's *Neopolitics: American political ideas in the 1980s* (1985). Keeping track of the neo-ization of political culture is almost as hard as keeping track of the post-ization of intellectual culture.

4   There are significant differences between the neo-conservative and moral traditionalist views of morality and the family. For the neo-conservatives, the family is private – outside the state's sphere of intervention. For the moral traditionalists, the state is the agency through which 'proper' private behaviour can be enforced. See Eisenstein (1987) and Crawford (1980: 161–2). More generally, on the place of children and the family in New Right ideology, see Hunter (1988b).

5   This is a very fleeting engagement with an issue which repays much more substantial analysis of the linking of rhetoric, discursive strategies and performance in Reagan. See, *inter alia*, Grossberg (1988). Garrison Keillor's comments on Reagan as storyteller (1989: xviii–xix) are also suggestive.

6   It may be significant that the expansion of state employment benefitted black and women workers disproportionately, thus adding further dimensions of hostility towards the 'New Class'. Krieger observes that:

> Between 1969 and 1980 the social welfare economy (both government and private contract work) accounted for 39% of all new jobs for women, for black women it accounted for fully 58% of the jobs gained during this period. As a result, women, blacks, and especially black women have been disproportionately harmed by the reductions in force (RIFs) mandated by the cuts. (1987: 192).

The same issue is highlighted by Julianne Malveaux, and linked to the racial and gender recomposition of employment and poverty in the 1980s (Malveaux 1987). One of the key intellectual linkages of the New Class and neo-conservatism is the derivation of the concept from the writings of Milovan Djilas on the class structure of state socialist societies and the role played by bureaucratic power (1957).

7   The elucidation of this calculus includes a striking dismissal of the value of anthropological evidence about culture, which is ironic in the light of how cultural arguments come to play a central role in the later part of the book, for example, concerning status and sub-cultural distinctions between the working and non-working poor. Just as Marx was driven to comment on the 'bourgeois' character of the Robinson Crusoe story, so it is worth noting that Murray's capitalist calculus is 'naturalized' by an exemplary

tale about a farmer choosing between rice and jute cultivation (1984: p. 165).

8 In a comment directed at liberal hangovers among 'professional social analysts', Murray observes that, for them: 'the explanations are too *simple*, too unsubtle, to be true' (1984: 146). This echoes a Reagan comment that liberals 'claim there are no simple answers. There are simple answers, just no easy answers.'

9 See, for example, Hall (1988, 1989); and Levitas, ed. (1986).

10 Maddox and Lillie have argued that the social conservatism of many Democratic voters has long been in implicit tension with hostility towards the expansion of welfare and equality struggles associated with the Great Society elements of Democractic politics (1984).

11 Probably the best known – and largest scale – initiative was the Heritage Foundation's *Mandate for Leadership: Policy Management in a Conservative Administration*, a 3,000 page, 20 volume blueprint for the Reagan administration, produced in November 1980. In March 1982, the Heritage President, Edward J. Feulner, Jr., claimed that the Reagan administration had adopted 62 per cent of the report's 1,720 recommendations (Saloma 1984: 14–19).

12 This is not to argue that there exists either a natural anti-Reagan or a pro-left/liberal majority waiting to be discovered. The state of passive dissent also includes those demobilized from the political process in its entirety: suspended in cynicism, mistrust and disbelief. It might be argued that this state of political alienation owes as much to the nature of the process of political representation – intensified by what Davis has called the 'Californization' of politics and its conversion to permanent spectacle – as it does to the performance of particular political leaders. Perhaps a significant aspect of the Reagan appeal has been his ability, amidst this public cynicism about political performances, to perform sincerity.

6

Bringing it all back home: New Times and Old Enemies

The preceding chapters are linked by an effort to come to terms with what seem to me to be the central issues in contemporary cultural analysis. They emerged in the specific context of the USA, but their importance as both substantive features of contemporary culture and sites of significant theoretical arguments has a wider reach. My return to Britain involved a variety of culture shocks, but also underscored the salience of the issues I had been wrangling over while in the USA. Postmodernism has had a similar impact on intellectual vocabularies on both sides of the Atlantic, with equally discomforting consequences. The change from Reagan's America to Thatcher's Britain revealed similarly dispiriting parallels in the tone and tendency of political culture. And, in spite of exchanging dollars for pounds, the pleasures of consumption seemed to be where the action was – both practically and theoretically – in both countries.

None of this is too surprising. The patterns of increasing capitalist globalization and the particular dimensions of American economic, political and cultural hegemony over Britain within them mean that the discovery of similarities in the field of cultural analysis are to be expected. What these similarities did provide was the sense that I could get on and write about what had seized my attention whilst in the USA without trying to turn this into a book about 'America'. This feeling was given added emphasis by the increasing visibility of these same issues in debates within British cultural studies, debates directed towards analysing the changes in cultural formations in the 1980s. While trying to write I kept coming across arguments about where we were in the transition from modernity to postmodernity, the changing composition of class in Britain, the significance of consumption and the long reign of the New Right.

This set of issues has, individually and collectively, been the focus of much discussion but they were pulled together as the diagnosis of the contemporary state of Britain in an apparently unlikely context: the theoretical journal of the Communist Party, *Marxism Today*. I have used the words 'apparently unlikely' because throughout the 1980s the journal has tried to position itself as the vanguard of new thinking and analysis on the left rather than being the house journal of the Party. In particular, it championed the Gramscian analysis of the phenomenon of Thatcherism, publishing many of the articles which subsequently were collected in Stuart Hall's *The Hard Road to Renewal* (1989), for example. In 1988, the journal embarked on a project to define the major changes that were taking place in British society as the basis for rethinking political strategies on the left and published a variety of articles, comments and arguments under the umbrella heading of 'New Times'.[1]

Partly because of the symmetry of the issues between this book and the New Times analysis, and partly because New Times is marked by a strong cultural studies genealogy I have chosen to write this conclusion through an engagement with New Times rather to provide a more orthodox summation of the main arguments and general principles to be derived from the preceding chapters. This way of ending also serves two other purposes. First, it offers one way of 'bringing it all back home': of exploring the usefulness of arguments developed in one context (the USA) for understanding the peculiarities of another (Britain). Second, I hope that it embodies something of the approach to cultural studies that I inherited: which is that there are no final conclusions no grand theoretical principles to be enunciated. All work is work-in-progress and what follows it are more arguments. Consequently, this conclusion explores the main dimensions of the analysis of New Times and draws on the arguments of the earlier chapters as a basis for assessing its diagnosis of the 'present conjuncture'.

New Times represents an attempt to rethink Marxism in the face of economic, cultural and political changes which are seen as having outrun the analytical capacity of conventional Marxism. On the one hand, there is an attempt to describe these new times, to map the sets of changes taking place; on the other, there is a commitment to expand the means of analysis available, to develop a vocabulary of critical theory able to do justice to the study of these changes. New Times arises from a desire to overcome the multifaceted crisis of the left in Britain, which the protagonists see both as a central element of the current situation and as an obstacle to be overcome in the re-creation of left politics. The crisis of the left is inextricably linked to one of the overarching themes of 'New Times': the ten year hegemony of the New Right. The failures and limitations of one form of the left, social democratic politics/labourism, created a political terrain open to the subsequent exploitation by a populist New Right. The political and intellectual deformities of the left, its orientation toward white and male conceptions of activism and points of struggle, marginalized other possibilities of building counter-hegemonic politics. The intellectual limitations of an unmodernized and fundamentalist left meant little attention was given to the rapid social transformations that have reworked the face of British society or to the accomplishments of the New Right in transforming the field of politics.

The loosely integrated threads of New Times are an attempt to diagnose and cure this crisis by delineating the new social terrain on which the left must fight if it is not to be politically marginalized. New Times is committed to the modernization of the left – at least in intellectual terms – in a setting where the right has seized the future. The dominant signifier in the New Times analyses is *post-*: post-Fordist, postmodernist, post-labourist and, rather more ambiguously, post-Marxist. In their different spheres, these are the boundary posts marking the separation of old and new in the realignment of economic, political and cultural life. Dramatic though this array of 'posts' is, and pleasing though their symmetry must be to the cultural analyst, they are not the most precise signifier of the changes under discussion. A more accurate term would be 'different', since what is being described is the replacement of monolithic social arrangements by patterns of diversity. This stress on difference runs throughout the range of changes presented as parts of New Times – in economic organization, in consumer culture, and in politics. Here the collapse of the monolithic economic architecture of the Fordist factory, there the crumbling of the all powerful social democratic state.[2]

SCENE SHIFTING

It is possible to trace the impact of diversity across the entire social fabric. In the economy, change is signified by post-Fordism – the displacement of mass manufacturing by new technologies of production (Murray 1988). These have affected the process of production, the product and workplace organization. The process of production is disaggregated from the assembly line model: no longer integrated by the line but by new information systems.[3] These have allowed changes in the organization of work (for example the development of 'semi-autonomous work groups' and quality control circles) and in the nature of the product, moving away from the standardized output of mass production towards differentiated batch production within large scale manufacturing (of which Benetton clothing is the most often noted example). These changes in manufacturing, together with the secular decline of manufacturing itself and the rise of the service sector, have changed the character of the labour force: breaking the dominance of skilled white male labour, the spine of trade union organization. Together, changing sectoral distributions, changing technologies and changing employment practices have reorganized what used to be the core of labourism. In this way, post-Fordism in the economic domain is linked with what might be termed post-labourism in the political sphere. But post-Fordism is also linked to other sets of changes: this time in the cultural realm.

Diversity has come to be the dominant theme of consumer culture, fragmenting the apparent solidity of long-standing cultural formations into a shifting array of taste groupings, demarcated by the pursuit of difference. The diversity of production capability feeds into this fragmentation of taste and is also shaped by the growing dominance of the retail sector which now leads rather than follows the imperatives of production (Gardner and Sheppard 1989). New times are overshadowed by this consumerist orientation, both materially and symbolically. The influence of consumerism is pervasive: from the reconstruction of urban architecture around the shopping mall, through the growing salience of consumer research and advertising (the bastard twins of social science), to the overarching role played by the consumer in political rhetoric.

Here in the consumer culture, the relevant post is post-modernism: the detachment of signs from rooted meanings; the play of surfaces and images and the disengagement of the self from deeper structures. From postmodern architecture to rural nostalgia; from 'retro' fashion to recycled soul, the consumer culture sponsors a postmodern playfulness. But, in a slight frisson of uncertainty, New Times feels a little insecure with postmodernism: tempted by its deconstructionist and anti-monolith qualities, engaged by its celebratory and pleasure seeking stance and yet somehow resistant to its absolutist disengagement from politics and its liberation of the self from its moorings. A contradictory or even fragmented subject is one thing, the dissolution of the subject another matter entirely.[4] And so postmodernism's abolition of the subject is replaced by a sociology of new 'social and political subjects', through which the rationality, and meaningfulness, of the consumer culture is reconstructed through the lifestyle politics of these new subjects (for example Mort and Green 1988).

This concern with new social subjects restates the post-Fordist theme of diversity and the decline of uniformity. It highlights the emergence of gender, ethnicity and sexuality as arenas of cultural politics, creating new lifestyles and senses of self. These combine with other forces in cultural consumption (cosmopolitanism, youth subcultures, diversity of provision) to create a more self-conscious and self-orientated pattern of consumption. 'In addition, in recent years the social theatre of consumption has become more important. Choice in consumption, lifestyle, sexuality are more important as an assertion of identity. The dynamic area of most people's lives is where they can assert their difference from others.' (Leadbeater 1988: p. 15.)

Not surprisingly, these new subjects form a point of connection between cultural and political changes. Their emergence coincides with one aspect of the crisis of the left. Both 'labourism' and other traditions of organization on the left have been, at best, slow to respond to the emergence of new politics and, at worst, intentionally obstructive and exclusive. Feminism, the politics of race and sexuality have been held to the margins of orthodox left politics, viewed variously as diversions from, subsumable within, or 'natural constituencies' for, one form or another of the socialist project. New Times identifies these developments as forces for renewal, breaking the dependence of the left on a declining white/male/working-class conception of the basis of politics. The new forces are expansive in terms of of the terrain of politics, the style of politics, and the potential constituencies to be allied in progressive politics.

The crisis of the left is inextricably linked to the rise of the New Right – Thatcherism, in its specifically British version – not merely as the obvious corollary. The success of Thatcherism, especially in its populist realignment of politics, can be traced to its exploitation of failures of the left. Although this Conservative populism is a complexly woven ideology, two strands stand out in the New Times dissection of Thatcherism: its anti-statism and its rhetorical centrepiece of 'choice'. The two strands are, of course, not entirely separate since choice has provided one of the main axes of the Thatcherite critique of state power and its monopolistic character. This has focused on the institutions of public welfare: housing, health care and education; and has attacked them as concentrations of bureaucratic–professional power in the name of creating greater consumer choice. For New Times and others, Thatcherism managed to capture a mood of public resentment about the social democratic/labourist state. This attack on the oppressiveness of state institutions echoed earlier left critiques of the social democratic state: in particular, the concentration of bureaucratic and professional power and the effective disenfranchisement of users through a Fabian paternalism.[5]

The success of this anti-statism, both rhetorically and in its effective dismantling of aspects of state power (most visible in local government and education), together with its equally accomplished articulation of choice and consumer sovereignty, has provoked an extensive rethinking across the left about the possibilities of both learning from and countering the Thatcherite hegemony (for example Hall 1989). In part, these have explored the Gramscian concerns of the building of hegemony and its articulation with common sense. They have also examined alternatives to merely defending and promising to rebuild the social-democratic forms of state power. The success of choice has reintroduced the market to a role in left economic thinking; cast doubt on bureaucratic nationalization programmes as socialist building blocks, and promoted interest in the decentralization and democratization of state power as alternatives to market dominated conceptions of consumer choice (for example, Murray 1988; Mulgan 1988; Leadbeater, 1988).

Ideologically, these arguments are directed towards reclaiming the ground of common sense identified and dominated by Thatcherism. They aim at the disarticulation of choice and freedom from their economistic and individualistic inscriptions in the rhetoric of the New Right and their rearticulation into a left vocabulary as the basis for progressive alliances. Politically, the building of popular alliances (and popular forms of politics) is central to the New Times argument, because its diagnosis identifies the new with the breaking of one last monolithic structure: the class/party alignments of twentieth century British politics. Consequently, there can be no simple realignment of political forces in the old way (even if this were desirable). The changing composition of class, together with the emergence of new social subjects with diverse political agendas means rethinking the basis for counter-hegemonic politics, in which class is, at best, one of many identities.

New Times rests on the bifurcation of old (monolithic) and new (diverse) in a series of correspondences which link the economic, cultural and political domains. It is mirrored in the theoretical underpinnings of New Times, which are post-Marxist and oriented to the discursive analysis of difference. I do not mean to suggest that there is a single theoretical structure to New Times, since this would involve the erection of another monolith. But there is an overarching concern with the production of diversity which draws together strands from Foucault and the centrality of discourse, deconstructionism and fragments of postmodernism. The spirit of New Times ranges from Stuart Hall's Gramscian-inflected 'Marxism without guarantees' through Laclau and Mouffe's exploration of the construction of political subjects (1985), to a more postmodernist concern with the fragmentation of the social. Although differences are visible, there is a concerted movement away from old certainties (in particular, deterministic Marxism) towards a valorization of what might be called (in the language of the old certainties) 'the superstructures'.

Politics, ideology, culture and discourse are where the new action is (for example Mort and Green 1988), and even post-Fordism seems most interesting because of its intersections with culture and politics. The theorization of New Times is dominated by what Allen Hunter (1988c) has called a 'constructionist' approach, concerned with the production of social and political subjectivities, rather than the examination of identities and 'interests' embedded in social relations.

There is one other point to note about this dissection of the new. This is its predominantly celebratory and optimistic tone. The analysts of the new have found much to celebrate in the dissolution of the monolithic blocs of the past. The demise of (respectively) Fordism, Marxism, social democratic/labourist politics, a paternalist state, and ossified cultural forms is counted as a very small loss. What is equally striking is the commitment to reading these changes for their progressive possibilities. New Times identifies a field rich in prospects for the remaking of progressive politics, if only the last barriers of the old can be dismantled. Such new times require a new politics attuned to the economic, social and cultural diversity, one which can build a new collective political subject out of the plurality of subjectivities to replace the collapsing class-politics bloc of labourism. Such a new political subject cannot be a monolithic bloc but must be constructed from the multiple identities and potential constituencies which new times are creating. It requires an alliance which articulates different subjects, different agendas and different focal points of political concern and motivation.

THE OLD IN THE NEW

New Times has provided an invigorating contribution to the assessment of social change and its political consequences in modern Britain. Its attempt to construct a conjunctural analysis creates an important break from Marxist analyses which remain at the generalized level of systemic structure and the formal divisions of capital and labour. Nevertheless, there are some questions to be asked about New Times' diagnosis and prognosis. So far, there has been little by way of sustained criticism that works with the ideas being presented, rather than merely seeking to refute them at the 'systemic' level.[6] What follows is an attempt to assess the New Times by accepting its starting points for the evaluation of change.

Let us begin with the material base: the emergence of post-Fordism. This forms the central articulating concept, linking the reorganization of production and distribution to class recomposition, changing political forces and new patterns of consumption. For New Times, post-Fordism represents the emergent, if not empirically dominant, form of capitalist economic organization. However, this attribution of leading edge status leaves unanswered questions about the place of other forms of organization, not least Fordist systems themselves. By implication, these are relegated to residual status, to be eventually subsumed in the spread of post-Fordist patterns.

There must be some doubt as to whether the capital-intensive route of flexible specialization represents a viable strategy for all or even most capitals since the mass market-high turnover-low profit margins mode seems likely to continue as a central (if not the most visible) element of consumption. Thus, in electrical goods, clothing, toys, food, and even some aspects of the service sector, both pre-Fordist (labour intensive) and Fordist systems of production and distribution are likely to continue alongside the post-Fordist leading edge. For example, in retailing, 'sheds' such as Comet, MFI and Toys'R'Us coexist with boutiques, MacDonalds with Marks and Spencer food counters. Mike Rustin has argued that post-Fordist systems need to be seen not as a displacement of Fordist methods but as a new strategy taking its place in the repertoire available to capital in its attempt to manage crises of accumulation; a repertoire which will continue to include Fordist systems (1988: 58–61). Such a view of an enhanced repertoire of capital strategies includes paying more attention than the post-Fordist view to the tendential segmentation of the consumer market between the emergent taste/diversity and the residual low-cost/mass market sectors which reflect the deepening of labour market and income inequalities (see Bluestone and Harrison 1982).

Rustin highlights a more substantial theoretical problem in pointing to the way post-Fordism slides between referring to production processes and a wider analysis of the break up of the ensemble of economic, social and political relations which supposedly characterized the Fordist era. The latter is concerned with the dismantling of the balance of class power embedded in the postwar settlements between capital and organized labour, linked to an expanded and interventionist state. Defining the 'Fordist era' in such terms is a rather difficult enterprise, since Fordism and the expanded state are by no means co-terminous historically. In New Times, this disjuncture tends to be concealed by the 'analogy' between the monolithic nature of Fordist production and the monolithic nature of the expanded state. An equally substantial problem is that the restructuring of both capital and class formations has been only marginally dependent on the arrival of new techniques and technologies of production. In both Britain and the USA, the means to this end have included de-unionization, capital flight, the export of mass production methods, and political regimes with explicit anti-welfare and anti-union policy objectives (and rhetorics). New production methods have contributed (unevenly) to shifting this balance of forces, especially in the de-unionization of the workplace and drawing in new sources of labour, but its effect is relatively small by comparison with the consequences of selective de-industrialization, for example.

These arguments point to dangers in the use of the Fordism/post-Fordism couplet as a way of demarcating past from future, however attractive it might appear. At best it misidentifies the dimensions of change in class formation, and the major means of their accomplishment. More worryingly, the arguments by analogy to the realms of culture and politics (postmodernism and post-labourism) flatten patterns and processes of specificity into an oversimplified and ahistorical periodization. Not all of the protagonists of New Times share this reductionist tendency. Indeed, for many contributors, such an analysis is part of the problem which they seek to remedy. But even when attention turns to the specificity of the cultural and political domains, there are still some difficulties.

IN SEARCH OF SUBJECTS

The cultural equivalent of post-Fordism is postmodernism, loosely used to register the diversity of both cultural forms and social subjects (identities) which have proliferated in the last 20 years. Forms and identities are inextricably linked since identities are formed in and through elements of the cultural repertoire (that is to say, subjects are discursively constituted). The expansion of the national-popular culture – or, more accurately, the expansion of the cultural forms and symbols which make up its repertoire – has delivered an enhanced range of identities. The expansion creates more possibilities of differentiation and identities are manifested through chains of symbolic differentiation. This, and the diversity of social subjects which underlie such cultural differentiation, are reflected in, and refracted through, the marketing industry's concern to develop more and more sensitive market segmentation based on criteria of taste and lifestyle rather than on the outmoded patterns of socio-economic categorization.

This marketing approach finds a parallel in the increasingly voluntarist theorization of social subjects in post-Marxism. An initial emphasis on developing an alternative to determinist theories of consciousness (reflecting social relations in a direct and unmediated way) has given way to the discursive turn, in which subjects are formed in discourse. Here the categories of social position and social relations are, at best, marginalized and, at worst, expunged as laying illegitimate claim to an extra-discursive reality. Class is the primary, but by no means only, victim of this development, paralleling the dissolution of socio-economic categories in marketing. From the discursive stand-point, it is the constitution and articulation of subjects which is the focus of attention. Culture and politics are intimately linked in this view, as the discursive fields within which subjects are formed.

In New Times, this discursive turn is intimately linked to politics in two ways. On the one hand, the failure of the old class/politics model (in both its Marxist and labourist variants) is an essential component of the current situation, because of both its internal failures (that is class has not translated *automatically* into politics) and its external failures (that is its inability to engage with new social and political subjects, based on gender, sexuality, race and other 'non-class' dimensions). On the other hand, the articulation conception of politics is central to the dissection of the success of New Right politics in the form of Thatcherism, especially its ability to construct a new hegemonic bloc and to disarticulate older forms of political connection. However, I have some doubts about this view of the means of its success.

Where New Times has stressed the ideological (discursive) accomplishments of Thatcherism, the New Right itself has paid equal attention to the *material* conditions of hegemonic organization. There has been a systematic effort to ensure the material and institutional conditions appropriate to the liberating rhetoric, from which I want to identify four processes which are central to the changes discussed in New Times. The first of these bears directly on class politics in the sustained effort to reorganize the institutional bases of the postwar balance of class power. The ideological attack on the power of, and damage done by, trade unions has been supported by a series of legislative and judicial assaults on the organizational bases of unionism (membership rights, the right to strike, secondary picketing, mass picketing, and the sequestration of assets). This has provided the supporting infrastructure for an employers' offensive (including the state itself) directed at wage costs, staffing levels, working practices and, above all, at establishing the right of managers to manage.

Equally directed at the institutional points of attachment to labourism has been the long-term erosion of the public sector through economic and legislative means. Although all areas of the public sector have felt the impact of these assaults, the most striking area has been that of local government. The abolition of the Greater London Council and the metropolitan counties, rate capping, the transition to the Poll Tax, and the diminution of powers of local authorities in a range of fields, have aimed to destabilize local government as an institutional connection between class and politics in its labourist form. More abstractly, this can be viewed as an attempt to reorder the connections between civil society and the state in a more favourable direction by displacing the intermediate institutions which stand between the citizen and the national state (albeit citizens in their new guise as consumers). The reordering of power attendant on these changes has had a characteristic double movement – on the one hand, the greater centralization of power in the hands of Secretaries of State and their Departments (for example the national curriculum) and the decentralization of power to consumers and their proxies (for example local management of schools and the enhanced powers of school governors). The most direct disarticulation (in material as well as ideological terms) has been the selling off of council houses to council tenants, ensuring the spread of the property-owning democracy.[7]

The New Right's commitment to popular capitalism has been underwritten by the extensive programme of privatization wrought upon the public sector, aiming at a (however temporary) wider distribution of share ownership, and at dismantling the (however limited) conception of utilities such as gas, electricity and water as public goods. The 1980s have seen a systematic deconstruction of key areas of public relationships in an attempt to clear away the network of mediating institutions which interrupt a direct connection between the individual (and the family) and the state, making civil society approximate more closely to the ideal of the market place. This freeing of civil society has gone hand in hand with a fiscal policy directed to enhancing the role of private consumption alongside the decline in public consumption. Two aspects stand out in particular. Cuts in direct taxation (largely funded from de-linking some state benefits from wage or price inflation) have selectively increased personal disposable incomes; while the removal of credit restrictions has fuelled the massive expansion of personal consumption.[8] Consumers have to be made, not merely through discursive articulation, but through the reconstruction of material relationships.

While all these aspects of Thatcherism have been central to the 'ideological work' undertaken by the New Right, their transformative power needs to be seen as much in the process of disarticulating and re-articulating patterns of relationship: the material conditions which sustain particular forms of identity. It is true that, in general terms, the argument is made that discourses are embodied in institutional forms (regimes of subjection), the substantive analyses which have been developed have often taken the 'linguistic' discourse as the most accessible object of study with the institutional arrangements either lagging behind or being assumed to derive directly from the discursive constitution.[9] This relegation of institutional relationships is visible in much of the New Times analysis of new subjects and underscores the 'voluntarist' implications of articulation and disarticulation as political strategies (Hunter 1988c).

The political prescriptions of New Times bear the marks of this form of analysis. They are directed towards the construction of new political articulations of diverse social subjects in counter-hegemonic discourses. They stress learning from the success of Thatcherism, adapting to new social identities and the central task of articulating them in new directions (for example, towards a 'socialist individualism', Leadbeater, 1988). They also highlight the consumer as a modality of control and look to combine the consumer orientation (in its anti-paternalist implications for state forms) with regenerated models of citizenship and democratic control as alternative modes of address.

What is striking, though, is the material emptiness of these prescriptions. Although addressing the modes of relationship, they do not deal with what gives social subjects an investment in them. To do so, however, risks venturing onto the dangerous ground of labourism (or, even worse, Fabianism), already rejected for its statism and paternalism. Nevertheless, the issue of the real content of citizen's rights – the services which the state provides – is as significant as the constitutional conditions of those rights, or the modes of service delivery. But one looks in vain for indications of the conditions which might establish the material basis for a new variety of citizenship. These are the dull areas of Fabian reform such as the type, conditions and level of social benefits which create the basis for adequate social involvement; the provision of satisfactory housing; the equalization and improvement of health conditions; as well as the rather less Fabian concerns about combatting structural discriminations. The New Times critique of statism seems to have paralysed thinking about the state's material role in protecting and enhancing the conditions of public and private life. This is slightly strange since one of the signal failures of Thatcherism has been its inability to unlock the forms of attachment which large sections of the population have to selected aspects of the labourist state, the National Health Service, in particular. Such failures suggest that there remain deeply sedimented domains of 'common sense' which counter-hegemonic strategies could be colonizing, rather than assuming Thatcherism has mined all the available veins.

OPTIMISM OF THE INTELLECT AND THE REVENGE OF THE REPRESSED

The identification of new social subjects and their salience for political realignment is one of the most telling pieces of the analysis of the current situation. The development of new political groupings and potential groupings has created the possibilities of changing the political agenda for the left, and the critique of the failures of the left to come to terms with the politics of gender, race and sexuality is an important one. But even here, I have concerns about the perception of the diversity of social subjects and their political implications.

The enthusiasm with which New Times has greeted the 'new' subjects contrasts strikingly with its silence about what might be termed the 'old' subjects. Such groups are invisible both to the new Thatcherite ethos of radical individualism and to the New Times ethos of 'cultural politics'. Doubly excluded, they are 'invisible subjects': the constituencies and potential constituencies of old politics. The old, the state dependants, the low-paid, and the unorganized stand outside the charmed circle of the new. They are formed in the old ways with limited access to the pleasures of consumption: they neither work for, nor shop at, Benetton. Increasingly dependent on diminishing public sector provision and unable to exercise market choices in transport, housing, health, education and pensions, they are those at whom the 'services of last resort' are now targetted. For the New Right, they are marginal by virtue of their inability to participate in the market-place, and are rendered increasingly invisible by careful management of statistical returns of unemployment, health, and household income. For New Times, their absence from the new forms of both culture and politics seems to guarantee their invisibility. I find their disappearance especially puzzling given that, during the Thatcher decade, these patterns of economic and social inequality have deepened and that, within them, the interconnected webs of class, gender and race are most deeply woven (see, for example, Massey 1988).

In contrast to this New Times presents a determinedly optimistic reading of the new subjectivities available in the emergent national-popular culture. The celebration of choice, diversity and cultural politics as the basis for progressive rearticulations in politics seems to me an unnervingly one-sided assessment of the character of the national-popular. This is not to argue that the progressive potentials do not exist, but that they need to be set against the variety of forms in which regressive tendencies have deepened. The relative density of forms of sexism, racism, homophobia and virulent varieties of nationalism has increased during the 1980s across the entire field of popular culture. The recuperation of the dominant figures of heterosexual-white-male definitions of the nation has exacted cruel revenge on the limited liberal and radical gains of the 1960s and 1970s, and, in doing so, has increased the contradictoriness of popular culture.

Popular culture has been increasingly shaped by an overarching tension between a cosmopolitan expansionism and the retrenchment of the backlash. Against every gay presence has to be weighed the homophobic assault on the 'gay plague'; against every vestige of the 'new man' has to be set the deepening of an 'achievement-oriented' male culture (whose achievements range from occupational success to the commission of violence); against every hint of internationalism (in pop music, for example) has to be set the brute facts of an 'Argie ' (and the rest) bashing nationalism; and against the expansion of a black presence in the fields of popular culture has to be counted the continually deepening symbolic and real violence of racism.[10] Together with these revenges of the repressed one can also discern the return of symbolic forms of what might be termed 'classism' – the reconstitution of (apparently) archaic forms of hostility through the repertoires of accent, consumption and lifestyle.

While the reconstruction of the London Docklands has provided the most visible staging for the revival of class conflict in consumption, the reconstitution of symbolic class identities has been all pervasive and has taken a distinctly regressive form, that of the English gentleman and lady. The elementary forms of this identity are relatively simple to sketch: the house in the country, the Range Rover, the Barbour, the Wellingtons, caps and head scarves, 'county' accents resisting the dilution of received pronunciation by 'oikish' accents, and the rise of country pursuits. And, for all the 'diversity' of the market-place, the dominant imagery of men's clothing (and the shops through which it is purchased) has become that of the gentleman's outfitters. The 'new gentry' have thrived under Thatcherism and have celebrated by delineating a symbolic repertoire which registers their transcendence of the urban masses.[11] It is a cultural form which registers exactly the depth of the contradiction in popular culture – a powerful economic and stylistic impulse which is simultaneously the object of derisory humour ('okay, yah?' has become part of the comic repertoire).

In the context of such a contradictory field as popular culture, it requires a rather single-minded 'optimism of the intellect' to see this diversity of social subjects as the basis for a progressive political realignment. That 'traditional' forms of identity have been eroded and have been supplemented (though not supplanted) by new forms is a significant change, but New Times underestimates the extent to which this state of flux is being resolved into regressive combinations.

These regressive potentials become even more striking when one considers the forms of articulation between the contradictory fields of popular culture and political practice. The New Right has systematically sponsored and spoken for the regressive, rather than expansionist, combinations on offer in popular culture. The repertoire of nationalist, heterosexist, racist, masculinist symbolism, together with its celebration of privatized consumerism, form the dominant points of articulation between politics (both rhetorically and in practice) and popular culture. They are the aspects of common sense which Thatcherism has sought to both feed off and strengthen. At the same time, it has aimed at the marginalization and suppression of progressive strands of both traditional and emergent common sense. While New Times has underscored the salience of emergent strands based on new cultural and political forces, it has paid considerably less attention to the place of traditional elements, in particular the popular roots of labourism. Instead, its condemnation of the political form of labourism (the statist, bureaucratic, paternalist complex) has led to a dismissal of the social and cultural bases which both motivated and were managed by labourist politics.[12] Such traditional traces and sediments, although demobilized by the political realignments of the seventies and eighties, have nevertheless persisted as a passive political force resistant to the expansion of the would-be Thatcherite hegemony. The 'welfarist' role of the state forms the central thread of these traditional conceptions. It embodies a persistent commitment to the social in the face of the hegemony of the individual, most obviously but by no means exclusively visible in the sustained commitment to the imagery of the National Health Service. New Times engages with new politics at the expense of thinking through the problem of bringing together both traditional and emergent strands of good sense and, in doing so, mirrors its lack of attention to those who are not new social subjects.

SECOND CLASS POST

The importance of 'New Times' is the way it has posed the problem of social change, asking us to confront the intellectual and political issues of responding to the shifting sands of the present without reverting to dogmatic assertion. It does, however, create a difficulty for those who wish to present criticisms and bring up fundamental problems without being dismissed as 'fundamentalist'. In the preceding sections, I have tried to take New Times on its own terms as the starting point for a discussion of the present rather than beginning from abstract theoretical judgements about its correctness.

Nonetheless, I think that the arguments I have been making add up to something more than a disagreement about the empirical detail of social change. I think they involve differences of theoretical orientation and political evaluation whose consequences affect the whole assessment of the present conjuncture. New Times returned me to two of the starting points for this book: the legacy of cultural studies and my reluctance to become postmodern. The relevance of these two points of reference is not surprising: New Times both draws on and develops the legacy of cultural studies and links its appraisal of the new to postmodernism, reflected in the bifurcation of the 'monolithic' past and the 'diverse' future. Somewhere along this transition from cultural studies to postmodernism (and its alter-ego, post-Marxism) I want to call a halt and defend a different version of the cultural studies legacy.

New Times emerges in this transition from Marxism to post-Marxism, and a more detailed reading would demonstrate the unevennesses of that transition among its contributors. More precisely, New Times is constructed in the spaces between the search for a non-deterministic Marxism (centred around the exploration of Gramscian ideas) and the development of the Foucauldian discourse of power and subjectivity. One can see the emergent dislocation of social relations and the terrains of culture and politics, in which the problem of determinism of social relations is displaced by the problem of 'constitution' through discourse. It will come as no surprise that I believe points of value have been lost in that displacement, and that it results in an over-politicized and voluntarist conception of the current situation. In what follows I want to set out the losses of that theoretical transition and underscore their relevance to the analysis of new – and old – times.

The starting point is an insistence on the importance of social relations. Not merely those of class, but a recognition that the structuring power of relations of class, race and gender has both formative – and limiting – qualities in relation to the domains of culture and politics. At a minimum, this involves a claim that such relations constitute the major lines of force in the development of a society, and the major nodal points of power around which struggles over its development are likely to occur. More expansively, the relations of class, race and gender, and the patterns of their intersection, need to be viewed, together with the practices of culture and politics, as constitutive of subjects. To use more archaic terminology, the 'imaginary relations' of ideology address positions and trajectories of social subjects which they do not themselves form. This is not to elevate social relations into the status of abstract and unchanging combinations, since, as I argued earlier, such formations and their intersections are dynamic: processes as well as relationships (see Chapter 3). To take one crude example, positions within the nexus of class, race and gender bear powerfully on the possible ways in which individuals can inhabit the identity of the consumer.

Beyond that, I share New Times' view of the significance of (national-popular) culture as the site of hegemonic struggle within which the potential identities of individual and collective subjects are fought over. But I am concerned that New Times consistently over-reads the degree of volatility and plasticity of identities and cultural forms and, as a result, overestimates the pace of cultural change while underestimating the place and weight of 'sedimented' forms, practices and conceptions. I have argued already that New Times pays insufficient attention to both the progressive and regressive aspects of the 'sedimented' forms of identities of British culture. This flows from an overly constructionist-constitutive view of hegemony and the field of culture. For my part, I think that the Gramscian perspective on hegemony involves an injunction to look at national-popular culture as a much more contradictory domain than appears in New Times. Those contradictions emerge around a number of different lines of force. The first involves the distinction between sedimented and emergent cultural forms already mentioned, with the need to consider how the old is articulated with the new. The second concerns Gramsci's distinction between the 'good' and 'bad' sense of common sense: the need to politically evaluate the field of cultural practices and forms of identity to assess where progressive political connections can be forged. Here I have argued that New Times had been forgetful of elements of sedimented good sense in the old social and cultural bases of labourism in its dismissal of the political forms of labourism. Finally, there is the necessity of assessing the political balance of forces – the lines of domination and subordination – within the field of national-popular culture. Here, too, I think New Times is over-hasty: over-estimating the degree of the New Right's colonization of the national-popular and underestimating the weight of older forms of subordination because of their lack of visibility in the present.

I think that this limited and overly optimistic view of hegemony results from the down-playing of the problem of thinking through the connections between social relations and hegemonic practices within New Times. The question of hegemony is posed in the intersection of social relations, culture and politics, but New Times is focused on the cultural and political elements of this intersection. Attention is concentrated on the articulatory processes of identity construction rather than on the struggles to articulate identities with positions in social relations. The result is, as I have tried to suggest, an excessively constructionist view of hegemony, accentuating the discursive constitution of subjects at the expense of other dimensions. So, for example, there is more attention to the active creation of 'new' political subjects than there is to the demobilizing work: that which disempowers opposition and renders dissent passive. In these terms, the most significant rhetorical figure of the New Right may not be the 'consumer' (its active creation), but the claim 'that there is no alternative' (its demobilizing effect).[13] Equally significant is the neglect of the material dimensions of hegemony. New Times had given excessive attention to the discursive dimensions of hegemony and, as a result, had neglected both the material concessions offered to subaltern groups to ensure their support and the dismantling or marginalizing of institutional sites of opposition. The political dominance of the New Right needs to be understood as emerging from a strategy which combines the ideological enhancement of the realm of private interests and the material erosion of the public realm in reorganizing the relationships between the state and civil society.

New Times has promoted the importance of 'conjunctural analysis' – the examination of the current situation in concrete detail – and this is to be welcomed. But I am left with a feeling that this is a somewhat one-sided appropriation of Gramsci's distinction between the 'organic' and the 'conjunctural' aspects of analysis, in that New Times seems to represent the conjunctural without the organic. That is, the purpose of conjunctural analysis ought to be the assessment of how the complex of forces and powers in the present situation relate to and affect the underlying and longer term tendencies (the organic movements) of the society. Even allowing for my disagreements about the conjuncture, New Times seems less certain about how to make the connection with the underlying tendencies: what is being accentuated by the dominant forces in the present and what is being resisted or held back?

At the heart of this problem is the economic remaking of Britain within the new pattern of the global economy. The effect of Conservative rule through the 1980s has been to accelerate a number of organic tendencies in British capitalism: its deindustrialization and simultaneous 'financialization' through its macroeconomic policies, especially the management of interest rates in the latter part of the decade. Attached to this is the greater internationalization of the British economy in a number of aspects: the increased outflow of capital; the restructuring of labour to make Britain more attractive as end point assembly and, to a lesser extent, manufacturing base; and the enhancement of the attractiveness of the British market for private consumption (through microeconomic policies). These shifts, together with the greater transfer of mass production to Third World economies and the rise of the service sector, are part of global trends of capital formation but their impact has been intensified by state policy directed towards sponsoring them.

Such tendencies outrun the conceptual range of post-Fordism (especially in its narrower sense of changing patterns of production), and highlight the complex reorganization of social relations that accompanies such trends. The dominant patterns seem to be the enlargement of the middle classes (reflecting the American experience), in particular those in the commercial sectors rather than attached to the state (which dominated the earlier expansion of the middle class in the 1960s and early 1970s). Alongside this is a substantial recomposition of the working class, marked by a shrinking 'core' labour force, surrounded by an expansion of marginal, part-time, casual work (in the service sector, particularly) and an enlarged reserve army of the unemployed. Such changes have worked in and through the axes of gender and race. The enlargement of the middle class has included a small expansion of women's participation in the professions, management and small business sectors – although their symbolic visibility outruns their actual presence and is deeply implicated in conceptions of a post-feminist era (Newman, forthcoming). The greater advances of women's employment have occurred in the non-core labour market and in the service sector, in particular (and including the revival of domestic service). Asymmetrical patterns in this gendered division of labour have, if anything, intensified. Women's average pay has declined in proportion to men's; the expansion of part-time female work has gone alongside an increase of the average length of the male working day. The gender distribution of

domestic labour has remained largely unmoved at the same time
as both a real and a rhetorical enlargement of family (that is
mothers') responsibilities in the retreat from public provision.
The recomposition of class has intensified the racial fractures
in the formation of Britain, reorganizing the lines of exclusion
and reinforcing the patterns of containment in the non-core and
unemployed sectors of the emergent labour market. For both
Asian and Afro-Carribean groups the combination of continued
and increased structural discrimination, not merely in the labour
market; their demobilization from forms of representational
politics; and a revitalized (and politically legitimized) nation-
alist/racist cultural formation has resulted in a greater intensity
and diversity of 'cultural politics' (Gilroy 1987).

Such restructuring seems to me to represent the organic
tendencies within the conjuncture of new times. While change
has certainly been marked, the dominant forces and trends
within such changes look all too familiar: old enemies, indeed.
The 'newness' of these new times is perhaps more visible in the
domains of culture and politics, although even here, the epochal
qualities of the changes seem rather overstated. While contemporary popular culture is marked by higher levels of diversity
and a higher degree of plasticity, its most striking feature is
the deepening of its contradictory qualities. The intersections
of progressive liberal and radical elements, often deriving from
the cultural politics of the 1970s, the consuming cultural cosmopolitanism of the 1980s and the revival of traditional values (in
their most regressive forms) do constitute a remarkable diversity,
and tend to render invisible other sedimented or traditional
formations which are not articulated through the market-place
as their primary institution. But they also constitute a national-
popular which is riven by antagonisms, and in which progressive
elements in both emergent and traditional formations are both
defensive and dispersed. Equally importantly, their characteristic
institutional focal points – the various aspects of the public realm
(both inside and outside the state) – are being displaced and
marginalized by the reworking of civil society into a 'purer'
individualist, familialist formation.

For me, these changes represent not the realignment around
the 'posts' of New Times but the profoundly uneven results
of a programme of selective 'modernization' combined with

selective 'traditionalization': a perfect example of what Althusser called 'a teeth gritting harmony'. Its effect is the creation of a profoundly unstable national formation – economically, socially and culturally. In its haste to align itself within the posts, New Times has grasped one side of these processes – the visible signs of change – at the expense of ignoring the presence of the old in the new. More problematically, it has celebrated the presence of diversity and difference without coming to terms with the problem (both analytical and political) of the totality: how to understand, and create, a 'unity in difference'.

THE LAST POST (SCRIPT)

It has taken me a long time to put this book together. It began in March 1986 and I am writing this postscript December 1990. If its arguments have a connecting thread, it may be the problem of how to come to terms with social, cultural and political change without assuming that the new has obliterated the old. When I came to the Open University in 1980, the first course I worked on (*An Introduction to Social Sciences*) posed the question for its students of how to assess the interrelationship of continuity and change, and the question still seems to me to be the most important one. As the various arguments in this book show, I think the question applies both to the society one is studying and to the theoretical means for carrying out such analyses: I want to hold on to the presence of the old in the new as much in the concepts being used as in the social processes being considered. It is difficult to avoid seeing change. Since I discovered cultural studies in 1972, I have had to watch the rise of the New Right and the rise of the shopping mall. Since I started writing this book I have seen the displacement of both Reagan and Thatcher and the dismantling of the Berlin Wall and the Soviet hegemony which stood behind it. Changes abound, but still leave old patterns in place. The difficulty is how to assess the articulations of new and old and their consequences. What are the effects of old formations of racism and nationalism within the new politics inaugurated by the New Right? What are the effects of old religious, ethnic and national cultural formations within the changing politics of Eastern Europe?

I do not suppose that this book provides a complete answer to the question of how to assess the intersection of continuity and change. It carries no claim to, or guarantee of, 'truth'. But, in this would-be postmodern world, I still want to lay claim to there being something between absolute truth and disconnected fragments. That something is the process of arguing – using arguments as steps towards clarifying what we think is important and as contributions to long running conversations about why things are as they are.

I can still remember vividly what prompted me to try to join in the conversations represented in this book. On a March evening in 1986, I was sitting in an office in the University of Wisconsin at Madison reading a recent postmodernist article. Its excesses induced in me both an intense emotional reaction and an intense physical discomfort – a genuine gut reaction. The result of that reaction has been this attempt to stake out my own political and intellectual commitments in relation to those of others, to translate gut reactions into something I can communicate. It may be that a book is a fairly stilted way of joining in a conversation, but it did give me time to think about what to say. And, having said it, I am now suffering from the usual conversational after-effect: the thought that 'I wish I had said this instead of that . . . ' Still, no matter how solid the appearance of a book may be, I am reassured by the last thought from my cultural studies legacy. It is, after all, only work in progress: the best I can do for now.

NOTES

This chapter owes much to conversations with Allan Cochrane, Mary Langan and Janet Newman.

1 Although focused around the publication of the Communist Party's document 'Manifesto for New Times' (1989), the discussion of these topics has a much longer history in the pages of *Marxism Today*, which devoted a special issue to the subject in October 1988. A number of the major contributions have also been published in Hall and Jaques, eds (1989), whose introduction discusses some of the problems of a 'one-sided' analysis of new times.
2 Although applied to systems of production, Fordism has been used to draw parallels between economic and political structures,

in particular the bureaucratic, paternalist form of the 'social democratic' state, for example, Murray (1988); and Mulgan (1988).

3 Geoff Mulgan (1988) has linked the emergence of 'flexible systems' together with devolutionary and decentralizing initiatives in economic processes to the dispersal of power, and has suggested analogies with non-centralizing forms of political organization: networks rather than hierarchies. Suggestive though it is, it does leave untouched the problems of coordination between decentralized entities.

4 Postmodernism is a key referent for New Times, but as an index of cultural dispersal rather than as a theory of disconnection. But the discovery of a plethora of new identities has tended to leave to one side the problem of their basis (as opposed to their constitution). Equally, the problem of the integration of diverse subjectivities into single subjects, both at the individual and collective level, has not been resolved. There is an unstated but pervasive assumption of the equivalence of all identities. See also Hebdige (1988).

5 Such critiques emerged in the field of social policy in the 1970s and their appropriation by the New Right, through such agencies as the Centre for Policy Studies, and the accompanying transmutation of the politics of control into the model of consumer choice has proved a source of difficulty. See, for example Clarke, Langan and Lee (1980); and Clarke (1982).

6 One honourable exception to this rule is Mike Rustin's extensive critique in *New Left Review* (1989). Rustin's article combines an interrogation of the analysis of New Times with suggestive comments on the connection between the interests of social strata whose skills involve symbolic manipulation and their enthusiastic endorsement of the symbolic domain as the dominant feature of New Times. He also raises questions about New Times' determination to 'modernize', a scepticism shared by Ellen Meiksins Wood in a brief contribution to *Marxism Today* (1989).

7 This double movement of power associated with 'decentralization' raises problems about the analysis offered by Geoff Mulgan (1988) which emphasizes the downward dispersal of power. But in both public and private sectors, devolution has tended to be accompanied by the development of new systems of centralizing control, and a judicious view of what powers can be surrendered in practice.

8 The dependence of the 'consumer revolution' on expanded credit (paralleling the link between 'affluence' and hire-purchase in the 1950s and 1960s) raises problems about the hidden side of expanded consumption (the very high levels of personal indebtedness and its consequences) and about its likely longevity.

9 The most infamous example of this problem appears in Foucault's *Discipline and Punish* (1978) where the institutional expression of the discourse of surveillance is Bentham's 'Panopticon': a design

for a prison which never materialized. Subject to Baudrillard's disagreement, texts do not exhaust reality.

10 Dave Hill (1989) presents a telling commentary on the articulation of racism, masculinity and nationalism through football in his examination of 'the John Barnes phenomenon'. More generally, Paul Gilroy (1987) offers a powerful examination of the centrality of racism for the formation of the national identity.

11 It may be that living in a home counties commuter village has sharpened my sensitivity to this particular formation (and its diluted variants), but it has been commented on by others (Massey 1988), and the commuter fringes of London do contain the highest concentration of the middle class.

12 The intensity with which New Times seeks to banish the old left has been commented on by Rustin (1989) and, with particular reference to the revival of trade union activism at the end of the 1980s, by Ellen Meiksins Wood (1989). In the process, the social roots of labourism have been written off through the dismissal of its political forms.

13 Of course, the Conservative success in 'demobilizing' also owes much to the disorganization of political opposition through the fragmenting of the Labour Party and the constant reorganization of the 'middle-ground' throughout the 1980s.

Bibliography

Adams, J. R. *Secrets of the Tax Revolt*. Orlando, Fla.: Harcourt Brace Jovanovich, 1984.

Althusser, L. *Lenin and Philosophy and other essays*. London: New Left Books, 1971.

Althusser, L. and Balibar, E. *Reading Capital*. New York: Pantheon, 1970.

Anderson, P. *Considerations of Western Marxism*. London: New Left Books, 1976.

Apple, M. (ed.) *Cultural and Economic Reproduction in Education*. Boston, Mass.: Routledge and Kegan Paul, 1977.

Baudrillard, J. *For a Critique of the Political Economy of the Sign*. St. Louis, Mo.: Telos Press, 1981.

Baudrillard, J. 'The ecstasy of communication'. In Foster, H. (ed.), *The Anti-Aesthetic: Essays on Postmodern Culture*. Port Townsend, Wash.: Bay Press, 1983.

Beechey, V. and Donald, J. (eds) *Subjectivity and Social Relations*. Milton Keynes and Philadelphia: Open University Press, 1985.

Bennett, T. Introduction: 'the turn to Gramsci'. In Bennett *et al.*, *Popular Culture*, pp. xi–xix, 1986a.

Bennett, T. The politics of the 'popular' and popular culture. In Bennett *et al.*, *Popular Culture*, pp. 6–21, 1986b.

Bennett, T. *et al.*, (eds) *Popular Culture and Social Relations*. Milton Keynes and Philadelphia: Open University Press, 1986.

Biskind, P. *Seeing is Believing: How Hollywood Taught us to Stop Worrying and learn to love the Fifties*. New York: Pantheon, 1983.

Bluestone, B. *et al.*, *The Retail Revolution*. Boston, Mass.: Auburn House Publishing, 1981.

Bluestone, B. and Harrison, B. *The Deindustrialization of America*. New York: Basic Books, 1982.

Braverman, H. *Labour and Monopoly Capital*. New York and London: Monthly Review Press, 1974.

Butsch, R. (ed.) *For Fun and Profit: the commercialization of leisure*. Philadephia: Temple University Press, 1990.

Centre for Contemporary Cultural Studies (CCCS) *On Ideology*. London: Hutchinson, 1977.

CCCS *Women Take Issue*. London: Hutchinson, 1978.

CCCS *Culture, Media and Language*. London: Hutchinson, 1980.

CCCS *The Empire Strikes Back*. London: Hutchinson, 1982.

Chambers, I. *Urban Rhythms: Music and Popular Culture*. Basingstoke: Macmillan, 1985.

Chambers, I. *Popular Culture: The Metropolitan Experience*. London and New York: Methuen, 1986.

Clarke, J. Taking politics seriously: Thatcherism, Marxism and Welfare. *Crime and Social Justice*, No. 18, pp. 46–52, 1982.

Clarke, J. Pessimism vs. Populism: the problematic politics of popular culture. In Butsch, *For Fun and Profit*, 1990.

Clarke, J. *et al.*, (eds) *Working-Class Culture: Studies in History and Theory*. London: Hutchinson, 1979.

Clarke, J. *et al.*, Social work: the conditions of crisis. In Carlen, P. and Collison, M. (eds) *Radical Issues in Criminology*. Oxford: Martin Roberston, pp. 178–95, 1980.

Clarke, J. and Critcher, C. *The Devil Makes Work: Leisure in Capitalist Britain*. Basingstoke: Macmillan, and Chicago and Urbana, Ill.: University of Illinois Press, 1985.

Clarke, J. *et al.*, *Ideologies of Welfare*. London: Hutchinson, 1987.

Conway, F. and Siegelman, J. *Holy Terror*. New York: Dell, 1984.

Coser, L. and Howe, I. (eds) *The New Conservatives*. New York: Meridian, 1977.

Crawford, A. *Thunder on the Right: the New Right and the Politics of Resentment*. New York: Pantheon, 1980.

Critcher, C. Sociology, cultural studies and the postwar working class. In Clarke *et al.*, *Working-Class Culture*, pp. 13–40, 1979.

Cronin, J. E. and Radtke, T. G. The old and new politics of taxation. In Miliband *et al.*, *Socialist Register 1987*, pp. 263–96.

Davis, M. *Prisoners of the American Dream*. London: Verso, 1986.

Davis, M. *et al.*, (eds) *The Year Left 2: Towards a Rainbow Socialism*. London: Verso, 1987.

Djilas, M. *The New Class*. London: Unwin, 1957.

Eisenstein, Z. Liberalism, feminism and the Reagan state. In Miliband *et al.*, *Socialist Register 1987*, pp. 236–62, 1987.

Ellsworth, E. Illicit pleasures: feminist spectators and *Personal Best*. In Roman *et al.*, *Becoming Feminine*, pp. 102–19.

Ewen, S. *Captains of Consciousness*. New York: McGraw-Hill, 1976.

Ewen, S. and Ewen, E. *Channels of Desire*. New York: McGraw-Hill, 1982.

Ferguson, T. and Rogers, J. The myth of America's turn to the Right. *Atlantic Monthly*, May, pp. 43–53, 1986.

Fitzgerald, T. The New Right and the family. In Loney, M. *et al.*, (eds), *Social Policy and Social Welfare*. Milton Keynes and Philadelphia:

Open University Press, 1983.

Foucault, M. *Discipline and Punish*. London: Allen Lane, 1978.

Fox, R. W. and Lears, T. J. (eds) *The Culture of Consumption*. New York: Pantheon, 1983.

Friedman M. and Friedman, R. *The Tyranny of the Status Quo*. Orlando, Fla.: Harcourt Brace Jovanovich, 1984.

Gardner, C. and Sheppard, J. *Consuming Passion: The Rise of Retail Culture*. London: Unwin Hyman, 1989.

Gilder, G. *Wealth and Poverty*. New York: Basic Books, 1981.

Gilroy, P. *There ain't no Black in the Union Jack*. London: Hutchinson, 1987.

Gramsci, A. *Selections from the Prison Notebooks*. London: Lawrence and Wishart, 1971.

Gross, B. *Friendly Fascism: the New Face of Power in America*. New York: M. Evans, 1980.

Grossberg, L. Rockin' with Reagan, or the mainstreaming of postmodernity. *Cultural Critique*, 1988.

Grossberg, L. *It's a Sin: Postmodernism, Politics and Popular Culture*. Sydney: Power Publications, 1989.

Gutman, H. *Work, Culture and Society in Industrializing America*. New York: Vintage Books, 1977.

Hall, S. Cultural Studies and the Centre: some problematics and problems. In CCCS, *Culture, Media, Language*, pp. 15–47, 1980.

Hall, S. Notes on deconstructing 'the popular'. In Samuel, R. (ed.) *People's History and Socialist Theory*. London: Routledge and Kegan Paul, pp. 227–40, 1981.

Hall, S. The toad in the garden: Thatcherism among the theorists. In Nelson, C. and Grossberg, L. (eds) *Marxism and the Interpretation of Culture*. Chicago and Urbana, Ill.: University of Illinois Press, pp. 35–57, 1988.

Hall, S. *The hard road to renewal*. London: Verso, 1989.

Hall, S. and Jefferson, T. (eds) *Resistance through Rituals*. London: Hutchinson, 1976.

Hall, S. *et al. Policing the Crisis*. Basingstoke: Macmillan, 1979.

Hall, S. and Jaques, M. (eds) *New Times: The Changing Face of Politics in the 1990s*. London: Verso, 1989.

Halsey, A. H. 'Provincials and Professionals: the British Postwar Sociologists'. *LSE Quarterly*, Vol. 1, no. 1. pp. 43–74, 1987.

Hebdige, D. *Subculture: The Meaning of Style*. London: Methuen, 1979.

Hebdige, D. The bottom line on Planet One. *Ten/Eight*, 19, pp. 40–9, 1985.

Hebdige, D. *Hiding in the Light*. London and New York: Routledge, 1988.

Hill, D. *'Out of his Skin': The John Barnes Phenomenon*. London: Faber and Faber, 1989.

Hogan, D. Education and class formation: the peculiarities of the Americans. In Apple, *Cultural and Economic Reproduction in Education*, 1982.

Hoggart, R. *The Uses of Literacy*. Harmondsworth: Penguin, 1958.

Hunter, A. The ideology of the New Right. In Union for Radical Political Economy, *Crisis in the Public Sector*, pp. 309–332, 1981.

Hunter, A. The role of liberal political culture in the creation of middle America. *University of Miami Law Review*, Vol. 42, no. 1, pp. 93–126, 1988a.

Hunter, A. *Children in the Service of Conservatism: Parent-Child Relations in the New Right's Pro-Family Rhetoric*. Legal History Program, Working Papers Series 2, University of Wisconsin-Madison, 1988b.

Hunter, A. Post-Marxism and the new social movements. *Theory, Culture and Society*, no. 17, 1988c.

Jameson, F. Foreword to Lyotard, J.-F., *The Postmodern Condition: A report on Knowledge*. Minneapolis, Minn.: University of Minnesota Press, 1984.

Jhall, S. *et al*. Magic in the marketplace: an empirical test for commodity fetishism. *Canadian Journal of Social and Political Theory*, Vol. IX, no. 3, pp. 1–22, 1985.

Johnson, R. Three problematics: elements of a theory of working-class culture. In Clarke *et al.*, *Working-Class Culture*, pp. 201–237, 1979.

Johnson, T. J. *Professions and Power*. Basingstoke: Macmillan, 1972.

Kaplan, C. The culture cross-over. *New Socialist*, pp. 38–40, November 1986.

Keillor, G. *We are Still Married*. London and Boston, Mass.: Faber and Faber, 1989.

Kerber, L. K. and Mathews J. (eds) *Women's America: Refocusing the Past*. New York: Oxford University Press, 1982.

Krieger, J. Social policy in the age of Reagan and Thatcher. In Miliband *et al.*, pp. 177–198, 1987.

Kroker, A. Television and the triumph of culture: 3 theses. *Canadian Journal of Social and Political Theory*, Vol. IX, no. 3, pp. 34–47, 1985.

Laclau, E. *Politics and ideology in Marxist theory*. London: New Left Books, 1977.

Laclau, E. and Mouffe, C. *Hegemony and Socialist Strategy: Towards a Radical Democratic Politics*. London: Verso, 1985.

Laing, S. *Representations of Working-Class Life, 1957–1964*. Basingstoke: Macmillan, 1985.

Langan, M. and Schwarz, B. (eds) *Crises in the British State, 1880–1930*. London: Hutchinson, 1987.

Leach, W. Transformations in a culture of consumption: women and department stores, 1890–1925. *Journal of American History*, Vol. 71, no. 2, pp. 319–342, 1984.

Leadbeater, C. Power to the person. *Marxism Today*, October 1988.

Lears, T. J. From salvation to self-realization: advertising and the therapeutic roots of the consumer culture. In Fox and Lears *The Culture of Consumption*, pp. 1–38, 1983.

Levitas, R. (ed.) *The Ideology of the New Right*. Cambridge: Polity Press, 1986.

Lewontin, R. *et al., Not in our Genes*. Harmondsworth: Penguin, 1984.

Lipsitz, G. *Class and Culture in Post-war America: A Rainbow at Midnight*. New York: Praeger, 1982.

Lyotard, J. F. *The Postmodern Condition: A Report on Knowledge*. Minneapolis, Minn.: University of Minnesota Press, 1984.

McDowell, L. and Massey, D. A Woman's Place?. In Massey, D. and Allen, J. (eds), *Geography Matters!* Cambridge: Cambridge University Press, 1984.

McRobbie, A. and Nava, M. (eds) *Gender and Generation*. Basingstoke: Macmillan, 1984.

Maddox, W. S. and Lillie, S. A. *Beyond Liberal and Conservative*. Washington, DC: Cato Institute, 1984.

Malveaux, J. The political economy of Black women. In Davis *et al., The Year Left 2*, pp. 52–72, 1987.

Marable. M. 'The contradictory contours of black political culture'. In Davis *et al., The Year Left 2*, pp. 1–17, 1987.

Marx, K. *Grundrisse*. Harmondsworth: Penguin, 1973.

Marx, K. *Capital: Volume One*. Harmondsworth; Penguin, 1976.

Massey, D. A new class of geography. *Marxism Today*, May 1988.

Medcalf, L. J. and Dolbeare, K. M. *Neopolitics: American Political Ideas in the 1980s*. New York: Random House, 1985.

Meiksins Wood, E. The vision thing. *Marxism Today*, August 1989.

Miliband, R. *et al.,* (eds) *Socialist Register 1987*. London: Merlin, 1987.

Milton, D. *The Politics of US Labor*. New York: Monthly Review Press, 1982.

Moody, K. Reagan, the business agenda and the collapse of labour. In Miliband *et al.* (eds) *The Socialist Register 1987*, pp. 156–66, 1987.

Mort, F. and Green, N. You've never had it so good – again!. *Marxism Today*, May 1988.

Mulgan, G. The power of the weak. *Marxism Today*, December 1988.

Muncie, J. *The Trouble with Kids Today*. London: Hutchinson, 1985.

Murray, C. *Losing Ground: American Social Policy 1950–1980*. New York: Basic Books, 1984.

Murray, R. Life after Henry (Ford). *Marxism Today*, October 1988.

Myers, K. *Understains: The Sense and Seduction of Advertising.* London: Comedia, 1986.

Nelson, C. and Grossberg, L. (eds) *Marxism and the Interpretation of Culture.* Chicago and Urbana, Ill.: University of Illinois Press, 1988.

Newman, J. Enterprising women: images of success in Thatcher's Britain. In Stacey *et al.*, *Off-centre, Feminism and Cultural Studies*, 1991.

O'Connor, J. *The Fiscal Crisis of the State.* New York: St. Martin's Press, 1973.

Palmer, J. L. and Sawhill, I. V. (eds) *The Reagan Record.* Cambridge, Mass.: Ballinger Publishing, 1984.

Peiss, K. *Cheap Amusements.* Philadelphia: Temple University Press, 1986.

Piven, F. F. and Cloward, R. A. *The New Class War.* New York: Pantheon, 1982.

Poulantzas, N. *State, Power, Socialism.* London: New Left Books, 1979.

Reich, R. *The New American Frontier.* Harmondsworth: Penguin, 1984.

Reisman, D. *The Lonely Crowd.* New Haven, Conn. and London: Yale University Press, 1961.

Renner, K. The service class. In Bottomore, T.B. *Austro-Marxism.* Oxford: Oxford University Press, 1978.

Roemer, J. *A General Theory of Exploitation.* Cambridge, Mass.: Harvard University Press, 1982.

Roman, L., Christian-Smith, L. and Ellsworth, E. (eds) *Becoming Feminine: The Politics of Popular Culture.* London, New York and Philadelphia: Falmer Press 1988.

Rosenzweig, R. *Eight Hours for What We Will.* Cambridge: Cambridge University Press, 1984.

Rothmeyer, K. Citizen Scaife. *Columbia Journalism Review*, pp. 41–50, July/August, 1981.

Rustin, M. The politics of post-Fordism, or the trouble with 'New Times'. *New Left Review*, no. 175, pp. 54–77, 1989.

Salamon, L. M. and Abramson, A. J. Governance: the politics of retrenchment. In Palmer and Sawhill *The Reagan Record*, pp. 31–68, 1984.

Saloma, J. S. *Ominous politics: The New Conservative Labyrinth.* New York: Hill and Wang, 1984.

Seller, M. The education of the immigrant woman, 1900–1935. In Kerber and Mathews *Women's America*, pp. 242–56, 1982.

Simon, W. E. *A Time for Truth*. New York: Berkley Books, 1979.

Stacey, J. *et al.* (eds) *Off Centre: Feminism and Cultural Studies*. London: Harper Collins, 1991.

Thompson, E. P. *The Making of the English Working Class*. London: Gollancz, 1963.

Tobias, S. and Anderson, L. What really happened to Rosie the riveter? Demobilization and the female labor force, 1944–47. In Kerber and Mathews *Women's America*, pp. 354–73, 1982.

Trachtenberg, A. *The Incorporation of America*. New York: Hill and Wang, 1982.

Turner, G. *British Cultural Studies: An Introduction*. London: Unwin Hyman, 1990.

Union for Radical Political Economics *Crisis in the public sector*. New York: Monthly Review Press, 1981.

White, F. C. and Gill, W. J. *Why Reagan Won*. Chicago: Regnery Gateway, 1981.

Willis, P. *Learning to Labour*. London: Saxon House, 1979.

Williams, R. *Towards 2000*. New York: Pantheon, 1983.

Wilson, C. P. The rhetoric of consumption: mass-market magazines and the demise of the gentle reader, 1880–1920. In Fox and Lears (eds) *The Culture of Consumption*, pp. 39–64, 1983.

Wilson, J. Q. *Thinking about Crime*. New York: Basic Books, revised edition, 1983.

Wohl, S. *The Medical-Industrial Complex*. New York: Harmony Books, 1984.

Wolff, R. and Resnick, S. Power, property and class. *Socialist Review*, no. 86, pp. 97–124, 1986.

Wright, E. O. *Class, Crisis and the State*. London: New Left Books, 1978.

Wright, E. O. *Classes*. London: Verso, 1985.

Wright Mills, C. *White Collar*. New York, Oxford and London: Oxford University Press, 1956.

Young, P. D. *God's Bullies*. New York: Holt, Rinehart and Winston, 1982.

Index